VOGUE® KNITTING

QUICK GIFTS

VOGUE® KNITTING
QUICK GIFTS

SIXTH&SPRING BOOKS
NEW YORK

SIXTH&SPRING BOOKS
233 Spring Street
New York, New York 10013

Library of Congress Cataloging-in-Publication Data
Library of Congress Control Number: 2007920930

ISBN-10: 1-933027-23-1
ISBN-13: 978-1-933027-23-4

Manufactured in China

1 3 5 7 9 10 8 6 4 2

First Edition, 2007

TABLE OF CONTENTS

INTRODUCTION

Never before has the saying "It is better to give than to receive" been truer! With this generous gift collection, you can happily take part in your favorite crafty pastime and then relish the moment that your heartfelt creation is met with bright eyes and a beaming, appreciative smile. Surely, there can be no greater reward!

The patterns inside come in all shapes, sizes, colors and skill levels, so every knitter can be a giver. Start simple with a classic Felted Scarf on page 72 or the colorful iPod Case on page 36, or broaden your horizons with the Baby Cardigan on page 27 that showcases an irresistible argyle pattern. Also featured are felting, embroidery, cables, Fair Isle and more, and thanks to easy-to-read instructions and clear diagrams, you can confidently try them all!

Quick Gifts showcases the gamut of creative ideas, and each project is designed to be just what the title boasts: quick! So whether you finish your Christmas shopping in August or on its snowy Eve, this book has a project for you. Plus, most of these offerings are small and sweet, making them conveniently portable.

With this wide-ranging collection on hand, that perfect present is just needle clicks away. So check your calendar, pick a lucky giftee and **KNIT ON THE GO!**

THE BASICS

The best presents come from the heart, and there's no better way to show you care than with a delightful handknit gift. With projects for knitters of all ages and skill levels, this book will soon become your go-to guide for every gift-worthy occasion. If you're a beginner, try the simple and charming Knitted Gift Box, or, if you're a seasoned pro, the Hat and Mittens Set will give you just the right amount of challenge. Even felting enthusiasts have a variety to choose from, with designs ranging from the straightforward Felted Scarf to the more complex Felted Tote. No matter what shape and style it comes in, your knitted gift is sure to be treasured by whomever receives it.

YARN SELECTION

For an exact reproduction of the projects photographed, use the yarn listed in the "Materials" section of the pattern. We've chosen yarns that are readily available in the U.S. and Canada at the time of printing. The Resources list on page 92 and 93 provides addresses of yarn distributors. Contact them for the name of a retailer in your area.

YARN SUBSTITUTION

You may wish to substitute yarns. Perhaps you view small-scale projects as a chance to incorporate leftovers from your yarn stash, or the yarn specified may not be available in your area. You'll need to knit to the given gauge to obtain the knitted measurements with a substitute yarn (see "Gauge" on the next page). Be sure to consider how the fiber content of the substitute yarn will affect the comfort and the ease of care of your projects.

To facilitate yarn substitution, *Vogue Knitting* grades yarn by the standard stitch gauge obtained in stockinette stitch. You'll find a grading number in the "Materials" section of the pattern, immediately following the fiber type of the yarn. Look for a substitute yarn that falls into the same category. The suggested needle size and gauge on the yarn label should be comparable to that on the "Standard Yarn Weight" chart (see page 13).

After you've successfully gauge-swatched a substitute yarn, you'll need to figure out how much of the substitute yarn the project requires. First, find the total

GAUGE

It is always important to knit a gauge swatch, and it is even more so with garments to ensure proper fit.

Patterns usually state gauge over a 4"/10cm span; however, it's beneficial to make a larger test swatch. This gives a more precise stitch gauge, a better idea of the appearance and drape of the knitted fabric, and a chance for you to familiarize yourself with the stitch pattern.

The type of needles used—straight or double-pointed, wood or metal—will influence gauge, so knit your swatch with the needles you plan to use for the project. Measure gauge as illustrated. Try different needle sizes until your sample measures the required number of stitches and rows. *To get fewer stitches to the inch/cm, use larger needles; to get more stitches to the inch/cm, use smaller needles.*

Knitting in the round may tighten the gauge, so if you measured the gauge on a flat swatch, take another gauge reading after you begin knitting. When the piece measures at least 2"/5cm, lay it flat and measure over the stitches in the center of the piece, as the side stitches may be distorted.

It's a good idea to keep your gauge swatch in order to test blocking and cleaning methods.

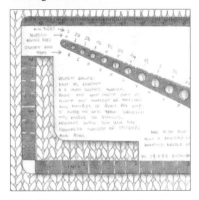

length of the original yarn in the pattern (multiply number of balls by yards/meters per ball). Divide this figure by the new yards/meters per ball (listed on the yarn label). Round up to the next whole number. The result is the number of balls required. Plastic bags can be used to hold the desired shape. If you choose to substitute yarn, be sure to knit and felt a test swatch.

FOLLOWING CHARTS

Charts are a convenient way to follow colorwork, lace, cable and other stitch patterns at a glance. *Vogue Knitting* stitch charts utilize the universal knitting language of "symbolcraft." When knitting back and forth in rows, read charts from right to left on right-side (RS) rows and from left to right on wrong-side (WS) rows, repeating any stitch and row repeats as directed in the pattern. When knitting in the round, read charts from right to left on every round. Posting a self-adhesive note under your working row is an easy way to keep track of your place on a chart.

COLORWORK KNITTING

Stranding

The Baby Cardigan on page 27 and the Tea Cozy on page 42 use the stranding method of colorwork. When motifs are closely placed, colorwork is accomplished by stranding two or more colors per row, creating "floats" on the wrong side of the fabric. This technique is sometimes called Fair Isle knitting, after the traditional Fair Isle patterns that are composed of small motifs with frequent color changes.

To keep an even tension and prevent holes while knitting, pick up yarns alternately over and under one another across or around. While knitting, stretch the stitches on the needle slightly wider than the length of the float at the back to keep work from puckering.

Stripes

Many of the projects in this book include stripes. Stripes can be worked with separate balls of each color. These strands are carried along the side of work when not in use. Be sure to keep an even tension of yarn not in use to prevent pulling.

SHORT-ROW SHAPING

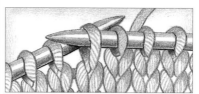

1 To prevent holes in the piece and create a smooth transition, wrap a knit stitch as follows: With the yarn in back, slip the next stitch purlwise.

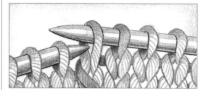

2 Move the yarn between the needle to the front of the work.

3 Slip the same stitch back to the left needle. Turn the work, bringing the yarn to the purl side between the needles. One stitch is wrapped.

4 When you have completed all the short rows, you must hide the wraps. Work to just before the wrapped stitch. Insert the right needles under the wrap and knitwise into the wrapped stitch. Knit them together.

Categories of yarn, gauge ranges, and recommended needle and hook sizes

Yarn Weight Symbol & Category Names	**1** Super Fine	**2** Fine	**3** Light	**4** Medium	**5** Bulky	**6** Super Bulky
Type of Yarns in Category	Sock, Fingering, Baby	Sport, Baby	DK, Light Worsted	Worsted, Afghan, Aran	Chunky, Craft, Rug	Bulky, Roving
Knit Gauge Range* in Stockinette Stitch to 4 Inches	27–32 sts	23–26 sts	21–24 sts	16–20 sts	12–15 sts	6–11 sts
Recommended Needle in Metric Size Range	2.25–3.25 mm	3.25–3.75 mm	3.75–4.5 mm	4.5–5.5 mm	5.5–8 mm	8 mm and larger
Recommended Needle U.S. Size Range	1 to 3	3 to 5	5 to 7	7 to 9	9 to 11	11 and larger
Crochet Gauge* Ranges in Single Crochet To 4 Inch	21–32 sts	16–20 sts	12–17 sts	11–14 sts	8–11 sts	5–9 sts
Recommended Hook in Metric Size Range	2.25–3.5 mm	3.5–4.5 mm	4.5–5.5 mm	5.5–6.5 mm	6.5–9 mm	9 mm and larger
Recommended Hook U.S. Size Range	B-1 to E-4	E-4 to 7	7 to I-9	I-9 to K-10½	K-10½ to M-13	M-13 and larger

*Guidelines only: The above reflects the most commonly used needle or hook sizes for specific yarn categories.

■□□□
Beginner
Ideal first project.

■■■□
Intermediate
For knitters with some experience. More intricate stitches, shaping and finishing.

■■□□
Very Easy Very Vogue
Basic stitches, minimal shaping, simple finishing.

■■■■
Experienced
For knitters able to work patterns with complicated shaping and finishing.

FELTING

Place knitted pieces in a top-loading or non-locking front-loading washing machine. Set to hot wash with low water level and add a small amount of detergent. Place the knitted item in a zippered pillowcase or mesh bag and put it in the machine with an old towel or two for agitation. Check the felting progress frequently as some yarns felt more quickly than others. It's a good idea to felt your gauge swatch as a test. Repeat the cycle, if needed, until the knitted pieces are felted to the desired size. Remove from washer and rinse gently in cool water to remove detergent. Roll the knitted pieces gently on a towel to remove excess water; do not twist or wring. Shape your item and let it air dry unless otherwise directed. You may stuff the felted item with plastic bags to hold the desired shape. If you choose to substitute yarn, be sure to knit and felt a test swatch.

BLOCKING

Blocking is a crucial finishing step in the knitting process. It is the best way to shape pattern pieces and smooth knitted edges in preparation for sewing together. If your project includes specific blocking or pressing instructions, be sure to follow them for best results. Most garments retain their shape if the blocking stages in the instructions are followed carefully. Choose a blocking method according to the instructions on the yarn care label, and when in doubt, test-block your gauge swatch.

Wet Block Method

Using rustproof pins, pin pieces to measurements on a flat surface and lightly

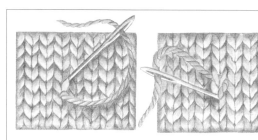 

DUPLICATE STITCH

Duplicate stitch covers a knit stitch. Bring the needle up below the stitch to be worked. Insert the needle under both loops one row above and pull it through. Insert it back into the stitch below and through the center of the next stitch in one motion, as shown.

dampen using a spray bottle. Allow to dry before removing pins.

Steam Block Method

With wrong sides facing, pin pieces to desired dimensions. Steam lightly, holding the iron 2"/5cm above the knitting. Do not press, or it will flatten stitches.

FINISHING

The pieces in this book use a variety of finishing techniques, from crocheting around the edges to embroidery. Refer to the illustrations for these and other helpful techniques.

CARE

Refer to the yarn label for the recommended cleaning method. To clean felted items, wash gently in cool water and take care not to agitate, which will cause the item to felt further.

FRINGE

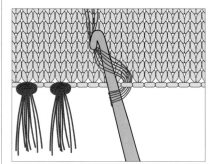 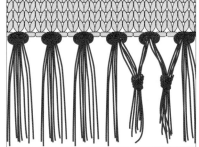

SIMPLE FRINGE: Cut yarn twice desired length plus extra for knotting. On wrong side, insert hook from front to back through piece and over folded yarn. Pull yarn through. Draw ends through and tighten. Trim yarn.

KNOTTED FRINGE: After working a simple fringe (it should be longer to allow for extra knotting), take one half of the strands from each fringe and knot them with half the strands from the neighboring fringe.

PROVISIONAL CAST-ON

The provisional cast-on, sometimes called open cast-on, is used when you want to have open stitches at the cast-on edge in order to pick up stitches later to work a hem, or if you want to weave these open stitches to the final row of stitches for a smooth seam. There are many different ways to work a provisional cast-on, two of which are described below.

With a crochet hook

1 Using waste yarn of a similar weight to the project yarn and a crochet hook appropriate for that yarn, chain the number of cast-on stitches stated in the instructions. Cut a tail and pull the tail through the last chain.

2 Using the needles and working yarn, pick up one stitch through the "purl bumps" on the back of each crochet chain. Be careful not to split the waste yarn, as this makes it difficult to pull out the crochet chain at the end.

3 Continue working pattern as described.

4 To remove waste chain, pull out the tail from the last crochet stitch. Gently and slowly pull on the tail to unravel the crochet stitches, carefully placing each released knit stitch on a needle.

Long Tail

1 Leaving tails about 4"/10cm long, tie a length of scrap yarn (approximately four times the desired width) together with the main yarn in a knot. With your right hand, hold the knot on top of the needle a short distance from the tip, then place your thumb and index finger between the two yarns and hold the long ends with the other fingers. Hold your hand with your palm facing upward and spread your thumb and index finger apart so that the yarn forms a "V" with the main yarn over your index finger and the scrap yarn over your thumb.

2 Bring the needle up through the scrap-yarn loop on your thumb from front to back. Place the needle over the main yarn on your index finger and then back through the loop on your thumb. Drop the loop off your

CIRCULAR NEEDLES

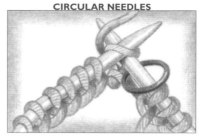

1 Hold the needle tip with the last cast-on stitch in your right hand and the tip with the first cast-on stitch in your left hand. Knit the first cast-on stitch, pulling the yarn tight to avoid a gap.

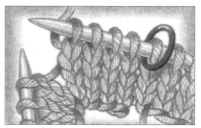

2 Work until you reach the marker. This completes the first round. Slip the marker to the right needle and work the next round.

thumb and, placing your thumb back in the "V" configuration, tighten up the stitch on the needle.

3 Repeat for the desired number of stitches. The main yarn will form the stitches on the needle and the scrap yarn will make the horizontal ridge at the base of the cast-on row.

4 When picking up the stitches along the cast-on edge, carefully cut and pull out the scrap yarn as you place the exposed loops on the needle.

DOUBLE-POINTED NEEDLES

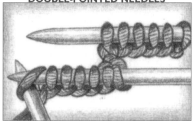

I Cast on the required number of stitches on the first needle, plus one extra. Slip this extra stitch to the next needle as shown. Continue in this way, casting on the required number of stitches on the last needle.

I With RS placed together, hold pieces on two parallel needles. Insert a third needle knitwise into the first stitch of each needle, and wrap the yarn around the needle as if to knit.

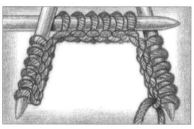

2 Arrange the needles as shown, with the cast-on edge facing the center of the triangle (or square).

2 Knit these two stitches together, and slip them off the needles. *Knit the next two stitches together in the same manner.

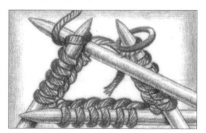

3 Place a stitch marker after the last cast-on stitch. With the free needle, knit the first cast-on stitch, pulling the yarn tightly. Continue knitting in rounds, slipping the marker before beginning each round.

3 Slip the first stitch on the third needle over the second stitch and off the needle. Repeat from the * in Step 2 across the row until all stitches have been bound off.

POMPOMS

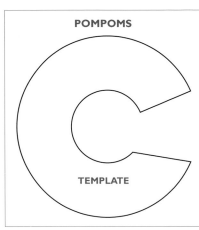

TEMPLATE

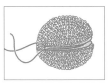

1 Following the template, cut two circular pieces of cardboard.

2 Hold the two circles together and wrap the yarn tightly around the cardboard several times. Secure and carefully cut the yarn.

3 Tie a piece of yarn tightly between the two circles. Remove the cardboard and trim the pompom to the desired size.

CROCHET STITCHES

CHAIN

1 Pass the yarn over the hook and catch it with the hook.

2 Draw the yarn through the loop on the hook.

3 Repeat steps 1 and 2 to make a chain.

SINGLE CROCHET

1 Insert the hook through top two loops of a stitch. Pass the yarn over the hook and draw up a loop two loops on hook.

2 Pass the yarn over the hook and draw through both loops on hook.

3 Continue in the same way, inserting the hook into each stitch.

SLIP STITCH

Insert the crochet hook into a stitch, catch the yarn, and pull up a loop. Draw the loop through the loop on the hook.

Illustrations: Joni Coniglio

EMBROIDERY STITCHES

STEM STITCH

LAISY DAISY

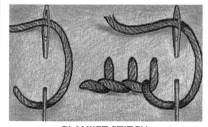

BLANKET STITCH

FRENCH KNOT

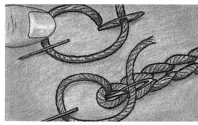

CHAIN STITCH

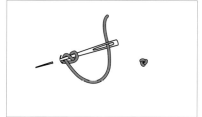

STRAIGHT STITCH

I-CORD

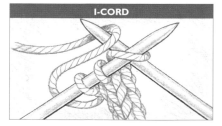

BUTTON HOLE STITCH

19

KNITTING TERMS AND ABBREVIATIONS

approx approximately

beg begin(ning)

bind off used to finish an edge and keep stitches from unraveling. Lift the first stitch over the second, the second over the third, etc. (U.K.: cast off)

cast on a foundation row of stitches placed on the needle in order to begin knitting

CC contrast color

ch chain(s)

cm centimeter(s)

cn cable needle

cont continu(e)(ing)

dc double crochet (U.K.: tr–treble)

dec decrease(ing)—reduce the stitches in a row (knit 2 together)

dpn(s) double-pointed needle(s)

foll follow(s)(ing)

g gram(s)

garter stitch knit every row. Circular knitting Knit one round, then purl one round

hdc half-double crochet (U.K.: htr–half treble)

inc increase(ing)—add stitches in a row (knit into the front and back of a stitch)

k knit

k f & b knit into front and back of stitch

k2tog knit 2 stitches together

k3tog knit 3 stitches together

knitwise (kwise) as if to knit

lp(s) loops(s)

LH left-hand

m meter(s)

M1 make one stitch—with the needle tip, lift the strand between last stitch worked and next stitch on the left-hand needle and knit into the back of it. One stitch has been added

MC main color

mm millimeter(s)

oz ounce(s)

p purl

p2tog purl 2 stitches together

p3tog purl 2 stitches together

purlwise as if to purl

pat pattern

pick up and knit (purl) knit (or purl) into the loops along an edge

pm place marker—place or attach a loop of contrast yarn or purchased stitch marker as indicated

psso pass slip stitch over

rem remain(s)(ing)

rep repeat

rev St st reverse stockinette stitch—purl right-side rows, knit wrong-side rows. Circular knitting: Purl all rounds (U.K.: reverse stocking stitch)

rnd(s) round(s)

RH right-hand

RS right side(s)

sc single crochet (U.K.: dc–double crochet)

S2KP slip 2 sts tog, k1, pass 2 sl sts over k1

sk skip

SKP slip 1, knit 1, pass slip stitch over knit 1

SK2P slip 1, knit 2 together, pass slip stitch over k2tog

sl slip—an unworked stitch made by passing a stitch from the left-hand to the right-hand needle as if to purl

sl st slip stitch (U.K.: single crochet)

ssk slip, slip, knit—slip next 2 stitches knitwise, one at a time, to right-hand needle. Insert tip of left-hand needle into fronts of these stitches from left to right. Knit them together. One stitch has been decreased

st(s) stitch(es)

St st stockinette stitch—knit right-side rows, purl wrong-side rows. Circular knitting: Knit all rounds. (U.K.: stocking stitch)

tbl through back of loop

tog together

tr treble crochet (UK: dtr–double treble)

WS wrong side(s)

w&t wrap and turn

wyif with yarn in front

wyib with yarn in back

work even continue in pattern without increasing or decreasing. (U.K.: work straight)

yd yard(s)

yo yarn over—make a new stitch by wrapping the yarn over the right-hand needle. (U.K.: yfwd, yon, yrn)

* repeat directions following * as many times as indicated

[ ] repeat directions inside brackets as many times as indicated

NECK WRAP

Eyelet necklet

■■■□

Give the gift of warmth with this lush neck warmer by Cecily Glowik. A perfect accessory for those chilly winter months, this quick knit features a beautiful eyelet pattern that looks like it took months to make.

■ Height 8"/20cm
■ Width 25"/63.5cm

MATERIALS

■ 3 1¾oz/50g balls (each approx 123yd/112m) Classic Elite Yarns *Lush* (angora/wool) in #4495 island plum **(4)**
■ One pair size 7 (4.5mm) needles *or size to obtain gauge*
■ Two ½"/1cm buttons

GAUGE

19 sts and 24 rows to 4"/10cm over eyelet pattern using size 7 (4.5mm) needles. *Take time to check gauge.*

EYELET PATTERN

(multiple of 3 sts plus 2)
Row 1 (RS) Knit.
Row 2 K1, *yo twice, k1; rep from *, end k1.
Row 3 K1, *[sl next st pwise wyib, drop both yos from previous row] 3 times, sl these 3 sts back to LH needle, [k3tog, p3tog, k3tog] tbl all into these 3 sts; rep from *, end k1.
Row 4 Purl.
Rep rows 1–4 for eyelet pat.

NECK WRAP

Cast on 38 sts. Work in eyelet pat until piece measures approx 25"/63.5cm from beg, end with row 4. Bind off.

FINISHING

Block piece to measurements.
Sew buttons on at 2½"/6.5cm up from cast-on edge and 2"/5cm in from side edges.

FELTED TOTE
Yikes, stripes!

Need the perfect gift for your favorite style maven? Kristin Omdahl's sophisticated handbag boasts a sturdy shape and a classic herringbone design that will thrill even the fussiest fashionista.

KNITTED MEASUREMENTS

- Approx 36"/91cm circumference and 18"/45.5cm tall before felting
- Approx 30"/76cm circumference and 12"/30.5cm tall after felting

MATERIALS

- 3 3½oz/100g skeins (each approx 190yd/174m) Brown Sheep Company *Lamb's Pride Worsted* (wool/mohair) in #M05 onyx (A) ⟨4⟩
- 2 skeins in #M10 creme (B)
- One size 10 (6mm) circular needle 24"/61cm long *or size to obtain gauge*
- One size 10 (6mm) straight needle for three-needle bind-off
- Contrasting scrap yarn for provisional cast-on
- Tapestry needle
- Mohair brush
- Two acrylic handbag handles 3"/7.5cm by 5"/12.5cm, style #30523 (available from www.mjtrim.com)
- ½yd/.5m imitation leather fabric for handle casings
- ½yd/.5m fabric for lining
- Sewing needle and black thread
- Stitch markers

GAUGE

16 sts and 24 rows to 4"/10cm over slip stitch pattern using size 10 needles before felting.

Take time to check gauge.

SLIP ST PATTERN

(multiple of 24 sts)

Rnds 1 and 2 With B, *sl 1, k2; rep from * to end.

Rnds 3 and 4 With A *k1, sl 1, [k2, sl 1] 3 times, k3, [sl 1, k2] 3 times, sl 1; rep from * around.

Rnds 5 and 6 With B *k2, [sl 1, k2] 3 times, sl 1, k1, sl 1, [k2, sl1] 3 times, k1; rep from * around.

Rnds 7 and 8 With A *sl 1, k2; rep from * around.

Rnds 9 and 10 With B *k1, sl 1, [k2, sl 1] 3 times, k3, [sl 1, k2] 3 times, sl 1; rep from * around.

Rnds 11 and 12 With A *k2, [sl 1, k2] 3 times, sl 1, k1, sl 1, [k2, sl 1] 3 times, k1; rep from * around.

Rep rnds 1–12 for slip st pattern.

BAG

With circular needle, provisionally cast on 144 sts (see page 16). Join to work in rnds, taking care not to twist sts on needle. Place marker for end of rnd. Knit 2 rounds. Work in slip st pattern until rnds 1–12 have been worked 9 times, work rnds 1 and 2 once more.

Next (turning) rnd (RS) With A *yo, k2tog; rep from * around.

Hem

Next rnd With A, knit.

Resume slip st pattern with rnd 5 and work to end of rnd 12. With A, bind off.

Base

Note Work base of bag with 2 strands of A held tog.

Carefully remove scrap yarn from provisional cast on, and pick up and knit the 144 sts with 2 strands of A.

Next rnd K48, pm, k24, pm, k48, pm, k24, pm.

Next (dec) rnd *K to 2 sts before marker, k2tog, slip marker, k2tog; rep from * around—136 sts.

Next rnd Knit.

Rep the last 2 rnds 11 times more—48 sts. Bend circular needle in half with 24 sts on each side. Use three-needle bind-off (see page 17) for all stitches.

FINISHING

Felting

Felt bag in washing machine (see page 14). Set bag out to dry overnight, inverted on something to hold its shape. Fold hem to WS at turning rnd, and sew in place with needle and thread.

HANDLE CASINGS

Cut two 6"/15.5cm lengths of leather fabric to fit the interior width of handles. Fold fabric in half over each handle for casings and place in center on either side of bag. Sew to hem on WS of bag.

BAG LINING

Cut lining fabric into 2 pieces, each approx 16"/40.5cm by 13"/33cm. With ½"/1cm seam allowance and 16"/40.5cm side as bottom edge, sew closed along 3 sides. Press back seam allowance along rem edge, place lining into bag and sew to hem on WS.

Using mohair brush, brush felted fabric in direction of zigzag designs.

BABY CARDIGAN

Prepping up baby

It s never too early to dress to impress. This colorful cardi by Michele Woodford is perfect for the wee one in your life.

SIZES
Instructions are written for 12 months. Changes for 24 months are in parentheses.

KNITTED MEASUREMENTS

- Chest 12½ (14¾)"/32 (37.5)cm
- Length 12½ (13¾)"/32 (35)cm
- Upper arm 9 (10)"/23 (25.5)cm
- Sleeve length from underarm 7½ (8½)"/ 19 (21.5)cm

MATERIALS

- 2 (3) 3½oz/100g balls (each approx 171yd/156m) Bernat *Cottontots* (cotton) in #90230 sweet green (MC)
- 1 ball each in #90421 strawberry (A), #90129 blue berry (B) and #90712 lime berry (C)
- One pair size 7 (4.5mm) needles *or size to obtain gauge*
- Tapestry needle
- Stitch holders
- Stitch markers
- Three ⅞"/22mm buttons in #1324 seaglass by Doodlebug Design Inc. (obtainable at www.doodlebug.ws)

GAUGE
18 sts and 24 rows to 4"/10cm over St st, using size 7 (4.5mm) needles, slipping the first st of every row. *Take time to check gauge.*

Notes

1 Pattern is written for a boy's sweater, with buttonholes worked on the left front band. For a girl's sweater, work buttonholes on right front band.

2 Sweater is worked with a selvage st (sel st) at each end of row to be used for seaming. Slip the first st of every row for sel st. Sel st is not included in measurements.

WRAP AND TURN
Work to designated stitch, slip st to RH needle. Bring yarn between needles to opposite side of work. Slip st back to LH needle. Turn work. 1 st is wrapped. Work to end of row, unless otherwise directed. Work the wrap tog with wrapped st when working across next complete row (see page 12).

SEED STITCH
(worked over an even number of sts)
Row 1 (RS) *P1, k1; rep from * to end.
Row 2 Purl the knit sts and knit the purl sts. Rep row 2 for seed st.

BACK
With MC, cast on 57 (69) sts.
Next row (RS) Sl 1(sel st), work to end in seed st.
Work 4 rows even in seed st with sel st.

Next row (WS) Sl 1(sel st), purl to end.

Work 4 rows even in St st with sel st.

Begin chart

Next row (RS) Sl 1 (sel st), work 6-st repeat of row 1 of chart across to last 2 sts, end with st 7, k last st in color just worked.

Next row (WS) Sl 1 (sel st), beg with st 7, rep row 2 of chart across to last 2 sts, end with st 1, k last st in color just worked.

Work even until 21 rows of chart have been completed.

With MC work even until piece measures 8 (8½)"/20.5 (21.5)cm from beg, end with WS row.

Shape armhole

Bind off 3 sts at beg next 2 rows—51 (63) sts.

Next (dec) row (RS) Sl 1, k1, ssk, work to last 4 sts, k2tog, k2—49 (61) sts.

Next row Sl 1, purl to end.

Rep last 2 rows 3 times more—43 (55) sts.

Work even until armhole measures 4¾ (5¼)"/12 (13.5)cm, end with WS row.

Next row (RS) Sl 1 (sel st), k6 (10), attach second ball of yarn and bind off center 29 (33) sts, k to end. Sl 7 (11) sts each side to st holders for shoulders.

LEFT FRONT

With MC cast on 31 (37) sts.

Next row (RS) Sl 1 (sel st), work to end in seed st.

Work 4 rows even in seed st with sel st.

Next row (WS) Sl 1(sel st), keep next 5 sts in seed st for front band, pm, purl across to last st, M1, k last st—32 (38) sts.

Next (buttonhole) row (RS) Sl 1, k25 (31), sl marker, k1, p2tog, yo, p1, k1, p1.

Next row Sl 1, work seed st band, sl marker, purl to end.

Work 2 rows even in St st with seed st band and sel st.

Begin chart

Next row (RS) Sl 1, beg with st 1, work 6-st repeat of row 1 of chart across to 1 st before marker, end with st 7, sl marker, work seed st band. Work even until 21 rows of chart have been completed. Work even with MC until piece measures 8 (8½)"/20 (21.5)cm from beg, AT SAME TIME work one more buttonhole 3"/7.5cm above first.

Shape neck

Next row (RS) Sl 1, work to 2 sts before marker, k2tog, sl marker, work third button hole in front band sts—31 (37) sts.

Next row (WS) Sl 1, work next 4 front band sts, wrap 6th st, turn. Work RS row on 5 front band sts, turn.

Next row (WS) Sl 1, work next 2 front band sts, wrap 4th st, turn. Work RS row on 3 front band sts, turn.

Next row (WS) Sl 1, work across 5 front band sts working wraps tog with wrapped sts, sl marker, purl to end.

Next row (RS) Sl 1, work to 2 sts before marker, k2tog, work 6 front band sts—30

(36) sts. Work 1 row even on WS.

Shape armhole

Next (dec) row (RS) Bind off 3 sts for armhole, k to 2 sts before marker, k2tog, work 6 front band sts—26 (32) sts.

Cont to dec 1 st at front edge every RS row 9 (11) times more and AT SAME TIME, work armhole shaping same as for back (ssk)—13 (17) sts. Work even until front measures same length as back, end with a RS row. Place sts on holder.

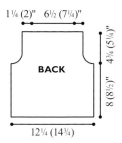

1¼ (2)"   6½ (7¼)"

BACK

4¾ (5¼)"

8 (8½)"

12¼ (14¾)

RIGHT FRONT

Work as for left front as follows: omit buttonholes, work 6-st front band and neck decs (ssk) at beg of RS rows and armhole shaping at beg of WS rows.

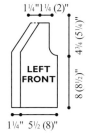

1¼"1¼ (2)"

4¾ (5¼)"

LEFT
FRONT

8 (8½)"

1¼" 5½ (8)"

SLEEVES

Cuff

With MC cast on 27 (31) sts.

Next row (RS) Sl 1 (sel st), work to end in seed st.

Work 4 rows even in seed st with sel st.

Next row (WS) Sl 1 (sel st), purl to end.

Next (inc) row Sl 1, M1, k across to last st, M1, k1—29 (33) sts.

Work 3 rows even in St st with sel st.

Work chart row 17, and inc 1 st each end of next row—31 (35) sts.

Work chart rows 18–21, then continue in MC, AT SAME TIME, inc 1 st each end of Row

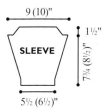

9 (10)"

1½"

SLEEVE

7¾ (8½)"

5½ (6½)"

21, then every sixth row 5 times—43 (47) sts.
Work even until sleeve measures 7¾ (8½)"/
19.5 (21.5)cm from beginning, end with
WS row.

Shape sleeve cap
Bind off 3 sts at beg next 2 rows—37 (41)
sts.
Next (dec) row Sl 1, k1, ssk, work to last
4 sts, k2tog, k2—35 (39) sts.
Next row Sl 1, p to end.
Rep last 2 rows twice more—31 (35) sts.
Bind off.

Lightly block all pieces to measurements.
Slip 7 (11) shoulder sts of each piece to
needles. With RS tog, join fronts to back
using three-needle bind-off (see page 17).
Back neckband
Slip 6 left front band sts to needles.
Next row (WS) Sl 1, work 5 front band
sts, inc 1 in last st for sel st—7 sts. Sl first
st of every row and work even until front
band measures to center of back neck edge.
Repeat on right front band. With RS of
neckbands tog, join using three-needle
bind-off. Sew neckband to back neck edge
using sel sts for seam. Set sleeves into armholes using sel sts. Sew side and underarm
seams using sel sts. With A, sew buttons to
front band opposite buttonholes.

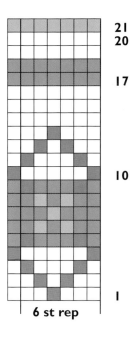

21
20

17

10

1

6 st rep

Color Key

□ MC

■ A

■ B

□ C

HAT AND MITTENS SET

Coffee and cream

■■■■▶

Who wouldn t love to slip on this matching set by Lois Young? The eye-catching stitch patterns are knit in a wool/alpaca blend, proving fashion and comfort go hand in hand.

Instructions are written for woman's size Medium.

MEASUREMENTS
- Mitten circumference 7½"/20cm
- Hat circumference 19"/47.5cm

Note Pattern is stretchy and will fit up to 24"/61cm head circumference.

MATERIALS
- 2 3½oz/100g balls (each approx 220yd/200m) Nashua Handknits/ Westminster Fibers Inc. *Creative Focus Worsted* (wool/alpaca) in #3249 chocolate (MC) 🄴
- 1 ball in #202 camel (CC)
- One size 6 (4 mm) circular needle 16"/40.5cm long *or size to obtain gauge*
- One set (4) size 6 (4mm) double-pointed needles (dpns)
- Cable needle
- Stitch markers
- Stitch holder
- Cardboard for pompom

GAUGE
26 sts and 32 rows to 4"/10cm in pattern stitch using size 6 (4mm) needles.
Take time to check gauge.

Notes
1 Sl all sts with yarn held to WS of work.
2 Change to dpns when circumference of hat becomes too small for circular needle.

STITCH GLOSSARY
6-st slip cable Sl next CC st to cn and hold to front, k2 MC, k CC st from cn, sl next 2 MC sts to cn and hold to back, k next CC st, k2 MC from cn.

Slip stitch cable pattern
(multiple of 8 sts)
Rnd 1 (RS) With CC *p1, k6, p1; rep from * to end.
Rnd 2 With CC *p1, sl 1, k4, sl 1, p1; rep from * to end.
Rnds 3, 4 and 5 With MC rep rnd 2.
Rnd 6 With MC *p1, 6-st slip cable, p1; rep from * to end.
Rep rnds 1–6 for slip st cable pattern.

HAT
With CC and circular needle, cast on 128 sts. Join, taking care not to twist sts. Place marker for end of rnd, sl marker every rnd. Work in slip st cable pat, rep rnds 1–6 nine times.

SHAPE CROWN
Rnd 1 With CC *p1, k1, k2tog, ssk, k1, p1, [p1, k6, p1] 3 times; rep from * to end—120 sts.
Rnd 2 With CC *p1, sl 1, k2, sl 1, p1, [p1, sl 1, k4, sl 1, p1] 3 times; rep from * to end.
Rnd 3 With MC *p1, ssk, k2tog, p1, [p1, sl 1, k4, sl 1, p1] 3 times; rep from * to end—112 sts.

Rnd 4 With MC *p1, k2, p1, [p1, sl 1, k4, sl 1, p1] 3 times; rep from * to end.

Rnd 5 With MC *[p2tog] twice, [p1, sl 1, k4, sl 1, p1] 3 times; rep from * end—104 sts.

Rnd 6 With MC *p2tog, [6-st slip cable, p2] twice, 6-st slip cable, p2tog; rep from *, replace marker for end of rnd—96 sts.

Rnd 7 With CC *p1, k1, k2tog, ssk, k1, p1, [p1, k6, p1] twice; rep from * to end—88 sts.

Rnd 8 With CC *p1, sl 1, k2, sl 1, p1, [p1, sl 1, k4, sl 1, p1] twice; rep from * to end.

Rnd 9 With MC *p1, ssk, k2tog, p1, [p1, sl 1, k4, sl 1, p1] twice; rep from * to end—80 sts.

Rnd 10 With MC *p1, k2, p1, [p1, sl 1, k4, sl 1, p1] twice; rep from * to end.

Rnd 11 With MC *[p2tog] twice, [p1, sl 1, k4, sl 1, p1] twice; rep from * end—72 sts.

Rnd 12 With MC *p2tog, 6-st slip cable, p2, 6-st slip cable, p2tog; rep from *, replace marker for end of rnd—64 sts.

Rnd 13 With CC *p1, k1, k2tog, ssk, k1, p2, k6, p1; rep from * to end—56 sts.

Rnd 14 With CC *p1, sl 1, k2, sl 1, p2, sl 1, k4, sl 1, p1; rep from * to end.

Rnd 15 With MC *p1, ssk, k2tog, p2, sl 1, k4, sl 1, p1; rep from * to end—48 sts.

Rnd 16 With MC *p1, k2, p2, sl 1, k4, sl 1, p1; rep from * to end.

Rnd 17 With MC *p2tog twice, p1, sl 1, k4, sl 1, p1; rep from * end—40 sts.

Rnd 18 With MC *p2tog, 6-st slip cable, p2tog; rep from *, replace marker for end of rnd—32 sts.

Rnd 19 With CC *p1, k1, k2tog, ssk, k1, p1; rep from * to end—24 sts.

Rnd 20 With CC *p1, sl 1, k2, sl 1, p1; rep from * to end.

Rnd 21 With MC *p1, ssk, k2tog, p1; rep from * to end—16 sts.

Rnd 22 With MC *p1, k2, p1; rep from * to end.

Rnd 23 With MC *p2tog; rep from * to end—8 sts.

Cut yarn, leaving 4"/10cm tail, pull through loops of sts to fasten off.

FINISHING
Make pompom in CC (see page 18). Attach to top of hat.

LEFT MITTEN

Cuff
With MC and dpns, cast on 48 sts. Divide evenly on 3 dpns. Join, taking care not to twist sts. Place marker for end of rnd, sl marker every rnd.

Rnd 1 P1, *k2, p2; rep from *, end p1. Rep rnd 1 14 times more.

Next rnd P1, *k2, p2; rep from * to last 3 sts, place marker for thumb gusset, k2, p1.

Next rnd With CC, p4, work next 16 sts in Rnd 1 of cable pat, p to end of rnd, and AT SAME TIME inc 1 st after gusset marker and before end-of-rnd marker—50 sts. Cont to work in rev St st (p every rnd) and cable pat, increasing as before every third rnd 3 times more—11 sts in gusset, end with rnd 4.

Rnd 5 Work around to gusset, put 11 gusset sts on holder, cast on 3 sts—48 mitten sts. Work even around 48 sts of mitten until rnds 1–6 of cable pat have been worked a total of 7 times, end with rnd 6.

Shape mitten top

Rnd 1 With CC p2tog, p2, [p1, k1, k2tog, ssk, k1, p1] twice, [p2, p2tog, p2tog, p2] 3 times, p2, p2tog—36 sts.

Rnd 2 P3, [p1, sl 1, k2, sl 1, p1] twice, p to end of rnd.

Rnd 3 With MC p2tog, p1, [p1, ssk, k2tog, p1] twice, [p1, p2tog, p2tog, p1] 3 times, p1, p2tog—24 sts.

Rnd 4 P3, k2, p2, k2, p to end of rnd.

Rnd 5 *P2tog; rep from * to end—12 sts.

Rnd 6 *P2tog; rep from * to end—6 sts.

Cut yarn, leaving 4"/10cm tail, pull through loops of sts to fasten off.

Thumb

Divide 11 gusset sts evenly on 3 dpns.

Next rnd With MC p 11 gusset sts, pick up and p 5 sts across 3 cast-on sts, place marker for end of rnd—16 sts.

[Purl 2 rnds CC, 4 rnds MC] twice, purl 2 rnds CC.

Top of thumb

Next rnd With MC *P2tog; rep from * to end—8 sts. Rep last rnd once—4 sts. Cut yarn, leaving 4"/10cm tail, pull through loops of sts to fasten off.

RIGHT MITTEN

With MC cast on and work 15 rnds as for left mitten.

Next rnd P1, k2, place gusset marker, work to end.

Next rnd With CC purl around to last 20 sts, work rnd 1 of cable pat over next 16 sts, p4, and AT THE SAME TIME inc 1 st after end-of-rnd marker and before gusset marker—50 sts.

Cont to work as established in rev St st (p every rnd) and cable pat, working gusset increases every third rnd 3 times more—11 sts in gusset, end with rnd 4.

Rnd 5 Work around to gusset, put 11 gusset sts on holder, cast on 3 sts—48 mitten sts. Work even around 48 sts of mitten until rnds 1–6 of cable pat have been worked a total of 7 times, end with rnd 6.

Shape mitten top

Rnd 1 With CC [p2, p2tog, p2tog, p2] 3 times, p2, p2tog, [p1, k1, k2tog, ssk, k1, p1] twice, p2tog, p2—36 sts.

Rnd 2 P21, [p1, sl 1, k2, sl 1, p1] twice, p3.

Rnd 3 With MC [p1, p2tog, p2tog, p1] 3 times, p1, p2tog, [p1, ssk, k2tog, p1] twice, p2tog, p1—24 sts.

Rnd 4 P14, [p1, k2, p1]twice, p2.

Rnd 5 *P2tog; rep from * to end—12 sts.

Rnd 6 *P2tog; rep from * to end—6 sts.

Cut yarn, leaving 4"/10cm tail, pull through loops of sts to fasten off.

Nano nano

Cute and colorful with just the right amount of sparkle, this stylish iPod nano case by Ruthie Nussbaum is an unexpected way to make a music lover smile.

KNITTED MEASUREMENTS

- Circumference 3½"/9cm
- Length 3½"/9cm

MATERIALS

- 1 1¾oz/50g skein (each approx 175yd/160m) Koigu *KPPPM* (wool) in #P147 rainbow
- One set (4) size 4 (3.25mm) double-pointed needles (dpns) *or size to obtain gauge*
- Size D/3 (3.25mm) crochet hook
- Stitch marker
- Tapestry needle
- ½"/1.5cm button with shank

GAUGE

28 sts and 40 rows to 4"/10cm over St st using size 4 (3.25mm) needles.
Take time to check gauge.

CASE

Cast on 24 sts. Distribute sts evenly on 3 dpns. Join to work in rnds, taking care not to twist stitches. Place marker for end of rnd.

Next rnd *K2, p2; rep from * around. Cont in k2, p2 rib for 4 more rnds.

Next rnd Knit around. Continue in St st until piece measures 3½"/9cm.

Distribute stitches onto 2 needles. Use three-needle bind-off (see page 17) to close bottom opening.

FINISHING

Sew button to center of one side at ½"/2cm down from top edge.

Button loop

With crochet hook, attach yarn to cast-on edge of case on side opposite marker. Ch 15, sl st in first st to form button loop.

Earbud loop

With crochet hook, attach yarn 1"/2.5cm below button. Ch 15, sl st in first st to form earbud loop.

KITTY TOY

Meow meow stripey pants

Precious and playful, Lucinda Guy's snuggly–soft cat doll is bundled up for the winter weather. Knit him up on a snowy afternoon, and he'll brighten your days (or those of a lucky someone) for years to come.

■ Height from toe to ear 12"/30.5cm

■ 1 1¾oz/50g ball (each approx 124yd/113m) of Rowan Yarns/Westminster Fibers, Inc. *Wool Cotton* (wool/cotton) each in #941 clear (MC), #962 pumpkin (A), #946 elf (B), #901 citron (C) and #908 inky (D) ⑧

■ One pair size 6 (4mm) needles *or size to obtain gauge*

■ One bag polyester fiberfill

■ Tapestry needle

23 sts and 31 rows to 4"/10cm over St st using size 6 (4mm) needles.
Take time to check gauge.

Row 1 (RS) With B knit.
Row 2 Purl.
Row 3 With C knit.
Row 4 Purl.
Rep rows 1–4 for stripe pattern.

(make 2)
With B cast on 22 sts.
Work in stripe pattern for 20 rows, AT SAME TIME inc 1 st each end on third row, then every fourth row 3 times more—30 sts. With A, work 6 rows in St st.
Next (dec) row (RS) K1, SKP, knit to last 3 sts, SKP, k1—28 sts.
Cont in A and St st, rep dec row every fourth row 3 times more—22 sts.
Purl 1 row.
Next row (RS) With A k1, SKP, k4, with MC k8, with a separate ball of A k4, SKP, k1—20 sts.
Next row With A p4, with MC p12, with A p4.
Next row With A k2, with MC k16, with A k2.
Next row With MC purl.
Cont in MC and St st for 30 rows, AT SAME TIME inc 1 st each end on next 2 RS rows—24 sts.
Bind off.

(make 2)
With A cast on 18 sts. Knit 1 row, purl 1 row.
Next row (RS) K5, SKP, k4, SKP, k5—16 sts.
Next row Purl.
Next row K4, SKP, k4, SKP, k4—14 sts.

Next row Purl.

Work even for 8 more rows.

With MC knit 1 row, purl 1 row.

Next row (RS) K3, SKP, k4, SKP, k3—12 sts.

Next row K3, SKP, k2, SKP, k3—10 sts.

Next row Purl.

Next row K3, [SKP] twice, k3—8 sts.

Next row (WS) [P2tog] 4 times—4 sts.

Next row [K2tog] twice, pass first st over second st—1 st.

Fasten off.

LEGS

(make 2)

With MC cast on 18 sts.

Knit 1 row, purl 1 row.

Next row (RS) K5, SKP, k4, SKP, k5—16 sts.

Next row Purl.

Next row K4, SKP, k4, SKP, k4—14 sts.

Work even for 5 more rows.

Next row K3, SKP, k4, SKP, k3—12 sts.

Next row Purl.

Next row K3, SKP, k2, SKP, k3—10 sts.

Next row Purl.

Next row K3, [SKP] twice, k3—8 sts.

Next row (WS) [P2tog] 4 times—4 sts.

Next row (RS) [K2tog] twice, pass first st over second st—1 st.

Fasten off.

TAIL

With MC cast on 18 sts.

Work even in St st for 28 rows.

Next row (RS) [K2tog] 9 times—9 sts.

Next row Purl.

Next row [K3tog] 3 times—3 sts.

Next row (WS) P3tog—1 st.

Fasten off.

EARS

(make 2)

With MC cast on 14 sts.

Knit 1 row, purl 1 row.

Next row (RS) K3, SKP, k4, SKP, k3—12 sts.

Next row Purl.

Next row K3, SKP, k2, SKP, k3—10 sts.

Next row Purl.

Next row K3, [SKP] twice, k3—8 sts.

Next row (WS) [P2tog] 4 times—4 sts.

Next row [K2tog] twice, pass first st over second st—1 st.

Fasten off.

SCARF

With B cast on 8 sts.

Work in stripe pat until scarf measures 18"/45.5cm, end with row 2.

Bind off.

FINISHING

Press all pieces on WS using a warm iron over a damp cloth.

With D follow diagram and embroider face onto one body piece for Front. With B make three large French knots (see page

19) for buttons on front, using photo as guide. With right sides of body pieces facing, sew together, leaving cast-on edges open. Turn RS out and fill with polyester fiberfill stuffing. Sew cast-on edges closed. In same manner, sew edges of arm piece; fill with stuffing; sew cast-on edge closed. Repeat with rem arm, leg, ear and tail pieces. Using the photo as a guide, sew arms, legs and ears to body. With D and using photo as guide, embroider paws with straight st (see page 19) onto front side of each arm and leg. Sew tail to lower back, securing well.

Sew scarf closed lengthwise. With seam on back of scarf, sew both ends closed. Press scarf lightly. With seam hidden, wrap scarf around Kitty's neck; sew in place.

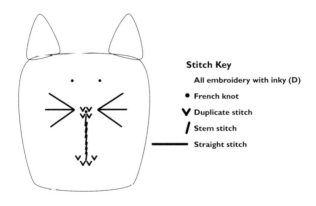

Stitch Key

All embroidery with inky (D)

● French knot

V Duplicate stitch

／ Stem stitch

——— Straight stitch

FAIR ISLE TEA COZY

One lump or two?

■ ■ ■ ▭

Teatime never looked so good. Knit up Micki Hair's vibrantly hued cozy for that Earl Grey enthusiast who always has the kettle on.

KNITTED MEASUREMENTS
■ Circumference 26"/66cm
■ Height 9½"/24cm

MATERIALS
■ 1 3oz/85g ball (each approx 197yd/180m) Lion Brand Yarn *Wool-Ease* (acrylic/wool) in #99 fisherman (MC), #102 ranch red (A), #171 gold (B), #174 avocado (C), #195 azalea pink (D), #107 blue heather (E) and #153 black (F) ④
■ Size 6 (4mm), 36"/91.5cm circular needle *or size to obtain gauge*
■ Size 5 (3.75mm), 36"/91.5cm circular needle
■ Size 6 (4mm) straight needle for three-needle bind-off
■ Stitch marker
■ Yarn needle
■ Cardboard for pompom

GAUGE
22 sts and 22 rnds to 4"/10cm in St st over chart using size 6 (4mm) needles.
Take time to check gauge.

Note When changing colors, twist yarns on WS to prevent holes.

STRIPE PATTERN
12 rnds C, *4 rnds B, 1 rnd E, 2 rnds D, 1 rnd E, 4 rnds B*, 1 rnd C, 10 rnds D, 1 rnd C. Rep from * to * once more, work to end in C.

COZY
With larger circular needle and MC, cast on 144 sts. Join, being careful not to twist stitches. Place marker for end of rnd. Purl 1 rnd, knit 1 rnd. Work rnds 1–58 of tea cozy chart in St st (k every rnd), working across both charts on pages 44–45.

FINISHING
Turn cozy inside out. Bend needle in half, 72 sts on each side. With one straight needle, work three-needle bind-off (see page 17) on WS.
Block lightly. Turn cozy RS out. Work embroidery (see page 19) following chart. To work French knots with F on strawberries, split yarn in half to use a 2-ply strand.

LINING
With RS facing, smaller needle and C, pick up 144 sts along cast-on edge. Join to work on rnds, place marker for end of rnd.
Next (dec) rnd Purl, dec 4 sts evenly spaced—140 sts. Work stripe pat in St st until piece measures the same length as cozy. Bind off. Fold lining in half lengthwise. Sew top of lining closed. Turn lining to inside of cozy, securing at corners.
With B, make two pompoms (see page 18), sew onto corners.

Tea Cozy Chart
Work across 144 sts

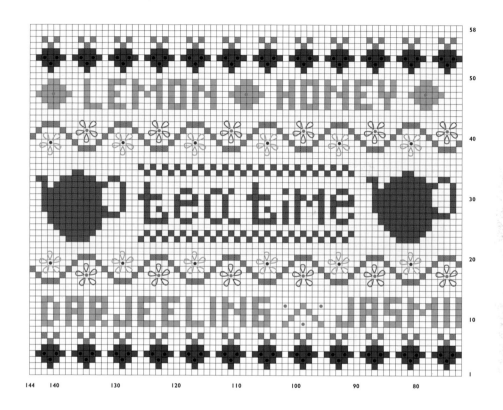

58

50

40

30

20

10

1

144   140   130   120   110   100   90   80

44

Color Key

☐ Fisherman (MC)

■ Ranch red (A)

■ Gold (B)

■ Avocado (C)

■ Azalea pink (D)

Embroidery Key

● French knot with black (F)

◉ French knot with ranch red (A)

◉ French knot with blue heather (E)

▽ Lazy daisy st with gold (B)

▽ Lazy daisy st with azalea pink (D)

Whether you're scaling a mountain or reaching for your Metrocard, your hands will stay warm and nimble in Micki Hair's fingerless gloves.

SIZES
Instructions are written for woman's size Medium.

KNITTED MEASUREMENTS
- Circumference 8"/20cm

MATERIALS
- 1 3½oz/100g ball (each approx 103yd/ 94m) Louet Sales *Gems Chunky* (wool) in #58 burgundy (A), #62 citrus orange (B), #17 shamrock (C), #49 charcoal (D), #26 crabapple (E), #15 neptune (F), #45 violet (G) and #42 eggplant (H) 🔵5
- One set (4) size 8 (5mm) double-pointed needles (dpns) *or size to obtain gauge*
- One set (4) size 7 (4.5mm) double-pointed needles (dpns)
- Stitch markers
- Yarn needle

GAUGE
18 sts and 24 rnds to 4"/10cm over Slip st pat using size 7 (4.5mm) dpns.
Take time to check gauge.

K1, P1 RIB
(worked over an even number of sts)
Row 1 *K1, p1; rep from * to end.
Repeat row 1 for k1, p1 rib.

SLIP ST PATTERN
(worked over a multiple of 18 sts)
Rnd 1 (RS) With B [k5, sl 1] 3 times.
Rnd 2 With B knit.
Rnd 3 With C k2, [sl 1, k5] twice, sl 1, k3.
Rnd 4 With C knit.
Rep rnds 1–4 for Slip st pat, following color sequence.

ABBREVIATIONS
M1L (make 1 left) Lift the bar between stitches so that the yarn goes from front to back over the needle. Knit into the back of this stitch so that it makes a loop when removed from the needle.

M1R (make 1 right) Lift the bar between stitches so that the yarn goes from back to front over the needle. Knit into the front of this stitch so that it makes a loop when removed from the needle.

GLOVE
Cuff
With smaller dpns and A, cast on 34 sts. Divide evenly over three needles being careful not to twist sts. Join and place marker for end of rnd, sl marker every rnd. Work in k1, p1 rib until piece measures 2½"/7cm.
Next rnd With larger dpns, knit, inc 3 sts evenly spaced—37 sts.
Hand and thumb
Note The hand is worked in Slip st pat, the thumb in St st. Slip markers every rnd.
Rnd 1 (RS) With B [k5, sl 1] 3 times, place thumb marker, M1L, k1, M1R, place thumb

marker, [k5, sl 1] 3 times—39 sts.

Rnd 2 With B knit.

Rnd 3 With C k2, [sl 1, k5] twice, sl 1, k3, k3 for thumb, k2, [sl 1, k5] twice, sl 1, k3.

Rnd 4 With C k18, M1L, k3, M1R, k18—41 sts.

Rnd 5 With D [k5, sl 1] 3 times, k5 for thumb, [k5, sl 1] 3 times.

Rnd 6 With D knit.

Rnd 7 With E k2, [sl 1, k5] twice, sl 1, k3, M1L, k5, M1R, k2, [sl 1, k5] twice, sl 1, k3—43 sts.

Rnd 8 With E knit.

Rnd 9 With F [k5, sl 1] 3 times, k7 for thumb, [k5, sl 1] 3 times.

Rnd 10 With F k18, M1L, k7, M1R, k18—45 sts.

Rnd 11 With G k2, [sl 1, k5] twice, sl 1, k3, k9 for thumb, k2, [sl 1, k5] twice, sl 1, k3.

Rnd 12 With G knit.

Rnd 13 With H [k5, sl 1] 3 times, M1L, k9, M1R, [k5, sl 1] 3 times—47 sts.

Rnd 14 With H knit.

Rnd 15 With A k2, [sl 1, k5] twice, sl 1, k2, remove thumb marker, place 11 thumb sts on holder, cast on 2 sts, k3, [sl 1, k5] twice, sl 1, k3—38 sts.

Rnd 16 With A k17, SKP, k2tog, k17—36 sts.

Rnd 17 With B [k5, sl 1] 6 times.

Rnd 18 With B knit.

Rnd 19 With C k2, sl 1, [k5, sl 1] 5 times, k3.

Rnd 20 With C knit.

Rnd 21 With D [k5, sl 1] 6 times.

Rnd 22 With D knit.

Rnd 23 With E k2, sl 1, [k5, sl 1] 5 times, k3.

Rnd 24 With E knit.

Little finger

Next rnd With E k4, slip next 28 sts to holder, cast on 1 st, k last 4 sts—9 sts. Knit 5 rnds. Bind off purlwise. Slip 28 sts back to larger dpns.

Next rnd With E knit 28, pick up and knit 1 st in little finger's cast-on st—29 sts. Knit 1 row.

Ring finger

Next rnd With F k5, slip next 19 sts to holder, cast on 2 sts, k last 5 sts—12 sts. Knit 6 rnds. Bind off purlwise. Slip 19 sts back to larger dpns.

Middle finger

Next rnd With G k5, sl next 10 sts to holder, cast on 2 sts, k last 4, pick up and knit 2 sts in ring finger's cast-on sts—13 sts. Knit 7 rnds. Bind off purlwise. Slip 10 sts back to larger dpns.

Index finger

Next rnd With B k10, pick up and knit 2 sts in middle finger's cast-on sts—12 sts. Knit 7 rnds. Bind off purlwise.

Thumb

Slip 11 thumb sts to larger dpns. With C k11, pick up and knit 2 sts in hand's cast-on sts—13 sts. Knit 5 rnds. Bind off purlwise.

■■■□

Dainty and dreamy, this mini slip stitch purse by Micki Hair is the perfect fit for that little shopper-in-training.

KNITTED MEASUREMENTS
- Knitted piece 9"/23cm wide by 16½"/42cm tall
- Finished purse 9"/23cm wide by 6"/15cm tall

MATERIALS
- 2 3½oz/100g skeins (each approx 225yd/206m) Claudia Hand Painted Yarns *Worsted* (merino wool) in stormy day (4)
- One pair size 5 (3.75mm) needles *or size to obtain gauge*
- One set (2) size 5 (3.75mm) double-pointed needles (dpns)
- One 1½"/3.75cm button (button shown is available from www.woolbearers.net)
- Stitch markers
- Yarn needle

GAUGE
22 sts and 32 rows to 4"/10cm over slip st pat using size 5 (3.75mm) needles.
Take time to check gauge.

Note
This pattern is worked with a selvage st (sel st) at each end that is knit every rnd to be used for seaming. Sel sts are not included in measurements.

SLIP ST PATTERN
(multiple of 6 stitches)

Row 1 (RS) *K5, sl 1; rep from * to end.
Row 2 Purl.
Row 3 K2, sl 1, *k5, sl 1; rep from *, end k3.
Row 4 Purl.
Repeat rows 1–4 for slip st pattern.

PURSE
Cast on 51 sts.
Knit 1 row, purl 1 row.
Next row (RS) K1 (sel st), work in slip st pattern across to last st, k1 (sel st). Work even until piece measures 6"/15.5 cm from beg, place markers on each end of row for bottom fold. Work even until piece measures 12"/30.5cm from beg, place markers on both ends for top fold. Work even until piece measures 14½"/37cm.
Next (buttonhole) row Work 24 sts, bind off 3 sts for buttonhole, work 24 stitches.
Next row Work 24 sts, cast on 3 sts, work 24 sts. Work even until piece measures 16½"/42cm from beg. Purl 1 row. Bind off.

FINISHING
Block piece lightly to measurements.
Assembly
Lay knitted piece flat with WS facing. Fold cast-on edge up to markers at 12"/30.5cm, creating bottom fold at 6"/15cm.Tack or pin side edges in place.

I-cord trim

Cast on 4 sts to one dpn. With front of piece facing, begin at lower left corner of bottom fold, *place dpn through both layers and pick up one st onto right end of dpn (next to working yarn tail) from back edge of piece—5 sts. Work 5-st attached I-cord as foll: slide stitches to opposite end of dpn, k3, k2tog through the back loops; rep from * along side edge to top fold. Do not bind off.

I-cord strap

Cont with 4 sts on dpn and work unattached 4-st I-cord (see page 19) for purse strap, until strap measures 48"/121cm. Pick up 1 st at right edge of top fold, and work in 5-st attached I-cord as before along side edge to bottom fold. Bind off.

Cast on 3 sts to one dpn. Pick up one st along cast-on edge and work in 4-st attached I-cord along inside edge of purse. Bind off. Cast on 3 sts to one dpn. Pick up one st at inside edge of top fold, and work 4-st attached I-cord along flap edge, easing around corners. Bind off.

Work buttonhole stitch (see page 15) around buttonhole, attach button.

BABY SET

Ahoy there, baby!

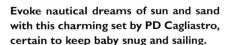

Evoke nautical dreams of sun and sand with this charming set by PD Cagliastro, certain to keep baby snug and sailing.

SIZES

Instructions are written for 6 months.

KNITTED MEASUREMENTS

- Chest 21"/53cm
- Length 11"/28cm
- Upper arm 9"/23cm
- Waist 22½"/57cm
- Leg 13½"/35cm

MATERIALS

- 2 1¾oz/50g skeins (each approx 190yd/174m) Cascade Yarns *Cherub DK* (nylon/acrylic) in #20 navy (A) and #34 tan (B) **(3)**
- Size 6 (4mm) circular needle, 20"/50.5cm long *or size to obtain gauge*
- One pair size 6 (4mm) needles
- One set (4) size 6 (4mm) double-pointed needles (dpns)
- Size G/6 (4mm) crochet hook

GAUGE

22 sts and 28 rows to 4"/10cm over St st using size 6 (4 mm) needles.
Take time to check gauge.

SWEATER

With A and circular needle, cast on 116 stitches. Join to work in rnds, taking care not to twist sts on needle. Place marker for end of rnd.
Next rnd *K1, p1; rep from * around.
Work even in k1, p1 rib for 1½"/3cm.
Next rnd Knit.
Knit 4 rnds B, 8 rnds A, 8 rnds B, 8 rnds A, 1 rnd B.

DIVIDE FOR FRONT NECK
Next rnd With B, k28, bind off 2, k to end—114 sts. Remove marker.
Working back and forth in rows, work even in St st for 6 rows more.

DIVIDE FOR ARMHOLES
Next row (RS) K26, bind off 4 sts, k54 for back, bind off 4 sts, k to end.

BACK
Join A to 54 back sts and work in St st for 5 rows.
With B work even in St st for 10 rows.
With A work even in St st until piece measures 9"/23cm from beg, end with WS row.
Shape neck
Next row (RS) K21, bind off 12 sts, k to end. Join second ball of A, working both sides of neck at same time, bind off 2 sts from both neck edges every other row 3 times—15 sts rem each side. Work even until piece measures 11"/28cm from beg. Bind off.

FRONT
Join sep balls of A to each side of front.

Working both sides at the same time, work even in same color sequence as back, until same length as back to the beg of neck shaping.

Shape neck

Cont in color sequence, and bind off 5 sts from both neck edges—21 sts each side. Bind off 2 sts from both neck edges 3 times—15 sts each side. When same length as back, bind off.

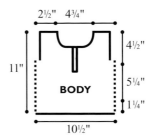

2½" 4¾"

11"

BODY

4½"

5¼"

1¼"

10½"

SLEEVES

With A and straight needles, cast on 36 sts.
Next row *K1, p1; rep from * to end.
Work even in k1, p1 rib for 1"/2.5 cm.
Next row (RS) Knit.

With A cont in St st for 11 rows more, then cont in B, AT SAME TIME, inc 1 st both sides every fourth row 7 times—50 sts. Work even until sleeve measures 6½"/16.5cm from beg. Bind off.

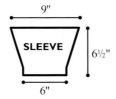

9"

SLEEVE

6½"

6"

FINISHING

Neck edging

Sew shoulder seams. Sew sleeve seams. Set sleeves into armholes. With crochet hook and B, beg at center back and sc loosely around entire neck edge.

Neck ties

With crochet hook and B, ch 40, attach to left front neck edge. Repeat, attaching to right front neck edge. Repeat twice more, attaching one tie to each side of front opening at approx 2"/5cm from neck edge.

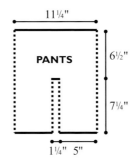

11¼"

PANTS

6½"

7¼"

1¼" 5"

PANTS

With circular needle and A, cast on 124 sts. Join to work in rnds, taking care not to twist sts on needle. Place marker for end of rnd.
Next rnd *K1, p1; rep from * around.
Work even in k1, p1 rib for 1"/1.5cm.
Knit 2 rnds.
Next (eyelet) rnd *K9, k2tog, yo; rep from * to last 3 sts, end k1, k2tog, yo.
Knit 2 rnds.
With B, work until piece measures 6½"/16.5cm from beg.

Divide for legs
Next rnd K27, bind off 8, k to last 35 sts, join second ball of yarn and bind off 8 sts, k to end   54 sts each leg.

Distribute 54 sts of one leg to 3 dpns, leave rem leg on needles to be worked later. Knit 7 rnds B, 8 rnds A, 8 rnds B, 12 rnds A, 6 rnds B, 2 rnds A.
Next rnd *K1, p1; rep from * around.
Next rnd *P1, k1; rep from * around.
Rep last 2 rnds twice more. Bind off.
Distribute rem 54 sts to dpns, working same as first leg.

FINISHING
Sew crotch opening closed.

Waistband tie
With crochet hook and B, ch 30"/76cm. Fasten off. Pull tie through eyelet holes in waist; tie in center front.

FRILLY SLIPPERS

Moca-socks

■■■■▶

Christine Walter's knit slippers are wonderfully warm and perfectly pretty, thanks to simple bows and feminine picot edging.

SIZES

Instructions are written for woman's U.S. size 8, European size 38½.

KNITTED MEASUREMENTS

■ Circumference 7¼"/18cm
■ Length 10"/25cm

MATERIALS

■ 3 1½oz/50g balls (each approx 105yd/96m) Cleckheaton/Plymouth Yarn Co. *Country Naturals 8-Ply* in #1835 teal tweed ③

■ Size 5 (3.75cm) circular needle, 16"/41cm long *or size to obtain gauge*
■ One set (5) size 5 (3.75mm) double-pointed needles (dpns)
■ Size G/4 (3.5mm) crochet hook

GAUGE

21 sts and 37 rows to 4"/10cm over double woven rib using size 5 (3.75mm) needles. *Take time to check gauge.*

DOUBLE WOVEN RIB

(multiple of 4 sts plus 2)
Row I (RS) K2, *sl 2 wyif, k2; repeat from * to end of row.
Row 2 Purl.
Repeat rows 1 and 2.

SLIPPER

Heel

With circular needle, cast on 20 sts.
Row I (WS) Sl 1 purlwise, purl across.
Row 2 (RS) Sl 1 knitwise, *k1, sl 1 purlwise; repeat from *, end k1.
Rep these two rows 12 times more for heel flap, rep row 1 once more.

Turn heel

Row 28 Sl 1 knitwise, k1, [sl 1 purlwise, k1] 5 times, ssk, k1, turn.
Row 29 Sl 1 purlwise, p5, p2tog, p1, turn.
Row 30 Sl 1 knitwise, k1, [sl 1 purlwise, k1] twice, sl 1, ssk, k1, turn.
Row 31 Sl 1 purlwise, p7, p2tog, p1, turn.
Row 32 Sl 1 knitwise, k2, [sl 1 purlwise, k1] 3 times, ssk, k1, turn.
Row 33 Sl 1 purlwise, p9, p2tog, p1, turn.
Row 34 Sl 1 knitwise, k1, [sl 1 purlwise, k1] 4 times, sl 1, ssk, k1, turn.
Row 35 P11, p2tog, turn—12 sts. Break yarn.

Gusset

With circular needle and RS facing, pick up and knit 13 sts in the slipped sts along left side of heel, knit across 12 heel stitches, pick up and knit 13 sts in the slipped sts along right side of heel—38 sts.

Instep

Next row (WS) Sl 1, purl to end.
Next row Sl 1, k1, *sl 2 wyif, k2; repeat from * to end of row.
Work even in double woven rib, slipping the first st of every row until 44 more rows

have been worked.

Next row (RS) Cast on 2 sts to LH needle, k4 and continue in pattern to end—40 sts. Slip sts evenly to 3 dpns, join to work in rnds. Place marker for end of rnd.

Next rnd (RS) Knit.

Next rnd K2, *sl 2 wyif, k2; repeat from * to end of row.

Next rnd Knit.

Rep these 2 rows until foot measures 8"/20cm or desired length from back of heel, end ready for knit rnd.

Toe

Rnd 1 *K2tog, k2; rep from * around—30 sts.

Rnd 2 *Sl 1 wyif, k2; rep from * around.

Rnd 3 Knit.

Rep rnds 2 and 3 three times more, then rnd 2 once.

Rnd 11 *K1, k2tog; rep from * around—20 sts.

Rnd 12 *Sl 1 wyif, k1; rep from * around.

Rnd 13 Knit.

Repeat rnds 12 and 13 once more, then rnd 12 once.

Rnd 17 *K2tog; rep from * around—10 sts. Break yarn, leaving an 8"/20cm tail. Using a tapestry needle, pull yarn through the remaining stitches on the needles and pull closed.

Cuff

With circular needle and RS facing, pick up and knit 23 sts along instep edge, 18 along heel, and 23 sts along instep edge—64 sts. Work in k1, p1 ribbing for 5 rows, end with a WS row. Knit 1 row. Resume k1, p1 ribbing for 8 more rows.

Next (bind-off) row K1, *p1, pass first st over second st on right hand needle, return last st to left hand needle, cast on 3 sts, bind off next 4 sts; repeat from *, end with p1, pass first st over last st.

Two hats, one heart

While Michele Woodford s cozy striped toppers make a charming offering for a lovestruck couple, don t resist the urge to gift them separately; these cashmere creations can stand on their own.

SIZES

Instructions are written for adult size Small. Changes for Medium and Large are in parentheses.

KNITTED MEASUREMENTS

- Circumference 19 (21, 23)"/48.5 (53.5, 58.5)cm
- Height 7½ (8, 8½)"/19 (20.5, 21.5)cm

MATERIALS

Woman s hat

- 2 (2, 3) ⅞oz/25g (each approx 70yd/64m) balls Schulana/Skacel Collection Inc. *Cashmere Trend* (cashmere) in #304 raspberry (MC) 🄵
- 1 ball each in #108 pastel yellow (A) and #107 gold (B)

Man s hat

- 2 (2, 3) ⅞oz/25g (each approx 70yd/64m) balls Schulana/Skacel Collection Inc. *Cashmere Trend* (cashmere) in #202 teal (MC) 🄵
- 1 ball each in #305 periwinkle (A) and #103 olive (B)
- Size 8 (5mm) circular knitting needle, 16"/41cm long *or size to obtain gauge*
- One set (4) size 8 (5mm) double-pointed needles (dpns)
- Stitch marker
- Tapestry needle

GAUGE

22 sts and 22 rows to 4"/10cm over rib pattern using size 8 (5mm) needles.
Take time to check gauge.

RIB PATTERN

(multiple of 11 sts)
Rnd 1 *K4, [p1, k1] 3 times, p1; rep from * around.
Rep rnd 1 for rib pattern.

HAT

With MC cast on 88 (99, 110) sts. Join to work in rnds, taking care not to twist sts. Place marker for beg of rnds.
Next rnd Work 11-st rep of rib pat 8 (9, 10) times around.
Work in rib pat for 7 rnds more.
With A work 4 rnds rib pat.
With MC work 2 rnds rib pat.
With B work 2 rnds rib pat.
With MC work even until hat measures 6 (6½, 7)"/15 (16.5, 18)cm.

SHAPE CROWN

Next (dec) rnd *K4, p1, ssk, k1, k2tog, p1; rep from * around—72 (81, 90) sts.
Next rnd *K4, p1, k3, p1; rep from * around. Work even for 3 rnds.
Next (dec) rnd *Ssk, k2tog, p1, k3, p1; rep from * around—56 (63, 70) sts.

Next rnd *K2, p1, k3, p1; rep from * around.

Work even for 3 rnds.

Next (dec) rnd *K2, p1, S2KP, p1; rep from * around—40 (45, 50) sts.

Next rnd *K2, p1, k1, p1; rep from * around.

Next (dec) rnd *K2tog, k1, ssk; rep from * around—24 (27, 30) sts.

Work 1 rnd even.

FINISHING

With yarn needle, pull yarn through rem sts several times, closing hole at top.

Trix are for knitters

Get creative with Tanis Gray's fun, multicolored necklace. Give it to that vivacious amiga who's always the life of the party.

KNITTED MEASUREMENTS
- Finished length approx 40"/101cm

MATERIALS
- 1 1¾oz/50g skein (each approx 183yd/167m) Brown Sheep Company *Nature Spun Sportweight* (wool) in #305 impasse yellow, #307 lullaby, #N54 orange you glad, #109 spring break, #207 alpine violet, #N60 purple splendor, #108 cherry delight and #N78 turquoise wonder **(3)**
- Contrasting scrap yarn for provisional cast-on
- One set (4) size 5 (3.75mm) double-pointed needles (dpns) *or size to obtain gauge*
- Size F/5 (3.75mm) crochet hook
- 1½yd/1.5m nylon fishing line
- Sharp tapestry needle
- Thirty-eight 1"/2.5cm styrofoam balls (available at www.save-on crafts.com)

GAUGE
22 sts and rows to 4"/10 sm over St st using size 5 (3.75mm) needles.
Take time to check gauge.

COLOR PATTERNS
Using color combinations of your choice, make 7 single-color balls, 6 two-color striped balls and 6 colorblock balls. Using photo as inspiration, make 19 randomly striped balls.

Two-color balls
(using any colors for A and B)
Rnd 1 With A knit.
Rnd 2 With B knit.
Rep rows 1 and 2.

Colorblock balls
(using any colors for A and B)
Rnds 1–5 With A knit.
Rnds 6–10 With B knit.

KNITTED BALLS
(make 38, no two alike)
Using provisional cast-on (see page 16), cast on 16 sts and distribute over 3 needles. Join to work in rnds, taking care not to twist sts. Place marker for end of end. Work in desired pattern and St st for 10 rnds. Break yarn, leaving 10"/25cm tail. Thread tail through sts and pull tight. Knot securely and trim tail. Insert styrofoam ball, with knot on WS of ball. Remove provisional cast-on, place sts on one dpn. Thread tail through sts and pull tight. Knot securely and trim tail, with knot on WS of ball. With nylon fishing line on tapestry needle, insert from top to bottom through center of each ball and string in desired order. Knot nylon line securely and trim ends.

■■■■□

Tee off in style with three different golf club cozies by Nancy Cassels. Take your pick from the ribbed cable, braided or eyelet designs, or knit all three for an attractive set.

- Length 8"/20cm
- Circumference approx 8"/20cm

- 1 3½oz/100g (each approx 233yd/205m) of Patons *Classic Merino Wool* (wool) in #77134 that's blue (A), #230 bright red (B) and #77023 camel (C) ▣
- One set (4) size 6 (4mm) double-pointed needles (dpns) *or size to obtain gauge*
- Cable needle
- Tapestry needle

20 sts and 28 rows to 4"/10cm over St st.
Take time to check gauge.

Cast on 44 sts, distributing over 3 dpns. Join to work in rnds, taking care not to twist sts. Place marker for end of rnd.

Ribbed cuff
Next rnd *K2, p2; rep from * around. Work even in rib for 4"/10cm.

Cozy top
Redistribute sts as foll: 10 sts on needle 1, 24 sts on needle 2, 10 sts on needle 3.

Next rnd K10 on needle 1, work rnd 1 of pattern st over 24 sts on needle 2, k10 on needle 3. Work even in St st and pattern st until piece measures 7½"/19cm from beg.

Shape top
Next (dec) rnd *K2, k2tog; rep from * around—33 sts.
Knit 2 rnds.
Next (dec) rnd *K1, k2tog; rep from * around—22 sts.
Knit 1 rnd.
Next (dec) rnd *K2tog; rep from * around—11 sts.
Break yarn and thread through rem sts, pull tight to close.

Stitch glossary
4-st LC Sl next 2 sts to cn and hold to front, k2, k2 sts from cn.
4-st RC Sl next 2 sts to cn and hold to back, k2, k2 sts from cn.

Pattern st
Rnds 1 and 3 K5, p2, k10, p2, k5.
Rnd 2 K5, p2, k2, [4-st LC] twice, p2, k5.
Rnd 4 K5, p2, [4-st RC] twice, k2, p2, k5.
Rep rnds 1–4.
With A cast on and work basic cozy, working pattern st on needle 2.

Pattern st
Rnd 1 K5, p2, yo, k3, SKP, k2tog, k3, yo, p2, k5.

Rnds 2, 4 and 6 K5, p2, k10, p2, k5.

Rnd 3 K5, p2, k1, yo, k2, SKP, k2tog, k2, yo, k1, p2, k5.

Rnd 5 K5, p2, k2, yo, k1, SKP, k2tog, k1, yo, k2, p2, k5.

Rnd 7 K5, p2, k3, yo, SKP, k2tog, yo, k3, p2, k5.

Rnd 8 K5, p2, k10, p2, k5.

Rep rnds 1–8.

With B cast on and work basic cozy, working pattern st on needle 2.

RIBBED CABLE COZY

Pattern st

Rnds 1–6 K3, p1, k1, [p2, k2] 3 times, p2, k1, p1, k3.

Rnd 7 K3, p1, sl next 4 sts to cn and hold to back, k1, p2, k1, [k1, p2, k1] from cn, sl next 4 sts to cn and hold to front, k1, p2, k1, [k1, p2, k1] from cn, p1, k3.

Rnds 8–10 K3, p1, k1, [p2, k2] 3 times, p2, k1, p1, k3.

Rep rnds 1–10.

With C cast on and work basic cozy, working pattern st on needle 2.

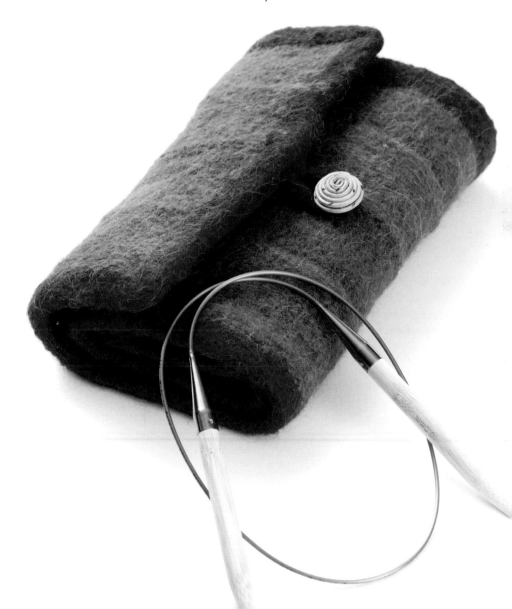

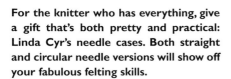

For the knitter who has everything, give a gift that's both pretty and practical: Linda Cyr's needle cases. Both straight and circular needle versions will show off your fabulous felting skills.

KNITTED MEASUREMENTS

Straight needle case
- 19½"/50cm wide by 21½"/55.5cm long before felting
- 16"/40.5cm square after felting

Circular needle case
- 27½"/70.5cm wide by 13"/33cm before felting
- 23"/58.5cm wide by 9"/23cm high after felting

MATERIALS

Straight needle case
- 2 3½oz/100g balls (each approx 127 yd/116m) of Classic Elite Yarns *Montera* (wool/llama) in #3887 pear (A) ④
- 1 ball in #3832 puma magenta (B)
- 1yd/1m fabric for lining
- Two 1"/25mm buttons

Circular needle case
- 2 balls #3885 bolsita orange (C)
- 1 ball #3858 cintachi red (D)
- ½yd/.5m fabric for lining
- One 1"/25mm button

Both
- One pair size 9 (5.5mm) needles, *or size to obtain gauge*
- Size G/6 (4mm) crochet hook
- Sewing needle, matching thread, sewing machine

GAUGE

16 sts and 22 rows to 4"/10cm over St st, using size 9 (5.5mm) needles before felting. *Take time to check gauge.*

STITCH GLOSSARY

Crocheted edging
Rnd 1 With RS facing, *work along cast-on edge and sl st in each st, work along side edge and sl st skipping every third st; rep from * along bound-off edge and rem side edge.

Rnd 2 Sc in each st around, working 3 sc in each corner st.

Rnds 3 and 4 Sl st in each st around.

STRAIGHT NEEDLE CASE

With A, cast on 79 sts. Work [30 rows St st, 30 rows rev St st] twice. Bind off.

Loops
(make 2)

With B and crochet hook, chain for 4"/10cm. Fasten off, tie ends together.

Edging
With B work crocheted edging around piece.

Felting
Felt all pieces in washing machine (see page 14). Tumble dry on high. Block with steam to shape.

Lining

Cut fabric to 29½"/75cm by 17"/43cm. Fold under and press ½"/1cm hem along both short edges. Topstitch across hem at ⅜"/1cm from folded edges. With topstitching on RS, fold one hemmed edge down 4"/10cm for top pocket, fold other edge up 8½"/21.5cm for lower pocket, adjusting to your felted piece if necessary. Fold under and press ½"/1cm hem along side edges. On lower pocket, sew vertical lines for channels as follows: 6 channels, each ⅞"/2.2cm wide; 4 channels, each 1⅛"/2.5cm wide; and 3 channels, each 1½"/4cm wide. Pin lining to felted piece. Pin loops along one side edge, between lining and felted piece, centering 5"/12.5cm apart. Hand-stitch lining in place, covering loop ends. Fold in thirds, with loops on top. Sew buttons in place to correspond to loops.

CIRCULAR NEEDLE CASE

With C, cast on 111 sts. Work [18 rows St st, 18 rows reverse St st] twice. Bind off.

Loop

With D and crochet hook, chain for 4"/10cm. Fasten off, tie ends together.

Edging

With D, work crocheted edging around piece.

Felting

Felt all pieces in washing machine (see page 14). Tumble dry on high. Block with steam to shape.

Lining

Cut fabric to 24"/61cm by 17"/ 43cm. Fold under and press ½"/1cm hem along both long edges. Topstitch across hem at ⅜"/1cm from fold edges. With topstitching on RS, fold one hemmed edge down 2"/5cm for top pocket, fold other edge up 5"/12.5cm for lower pocket, adjusting to your felted piece if necessary. Fold under and press ½"/1.5cm hem along side edges. On lower pocket, sew 5 vertical lines for pockets, each 3½"/9.5 cm apart. Pin lining to felted piece. Pin loop to center of one side edge, between lining and felted piece. Hand-stitch lining in place, covering loop ends. Roll up needle holder with loop on top. Sew button in place to correspond to loop.

Worn under a coat or displayed over a silk blouse, this beautifully embroidered scarf by Mags Kandis is sure to put stars in the eyes of its lucky receiver.

KNITTED MEASUREMENTS

■ 9¼"/23.5cm wide and 58"/147cm long before felting

■ 5"/13cm wide and 42"/107cm long after felting

MATERIALS

■ 3 1¾oz/50g balls (each approx. 105yd/96m) of Reynolds/JCA, Inc. *Lite-Lopi* (wool) in #442 royal blue (MC) **(4)**

■ Small amounts each in #264 mustard (A) and #444 grass (B)

■ One pair size 10½ (6.5mm) needles *or size to obtain gauge*

■ Tapestry needle

GAUGE

13 sts and 18 rows to 4"/10cm over St st (before felting).

Take time to check gauge.

SCARF

With MC, cast on 30 sts. Work in St st until piece measures 58"/147cm.
Bind off.

FELTING

Felt scarf in washing machine (see page 14), removing from machine when stitches are no longer visible. Pull scarf into shape and allow to dry flat.

FINISHING

If needed, press gently using steam.
Mark for a slit approximately 4"/10cm long down the center of the scarf starting approx 6"/15cm down from bind-off edge. Cut slit using sharp scissors. With photo as guide, follow diagram and work embroidery using B for spokes and A for French knots (see page 19).

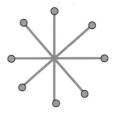

Stitch Key

● French knot with A

³/₄" straight st with B

Take a walk on the wild side with Amy Bahrt's super-cuddly animal pillows. Simple stockinette makes for a hassle-free knit while lovable details like button eyes and a moppy mane show you care.

KNITTED MEASUREMENTS
■ Body of each pillow 12"/30cm wide by 16"/41cm long

MATERIALS
Zebra
■ 3 1¾oz/50g skeins (each approx 137yd/125m) of Frog Tree Yarns *Merino* (wool) in #100 black (A) 🔲
■ 2 skeins in #0 natural (B)

Horse
■ 4 skeins in #7 brown (C)
■ 1 skein in #100 black (A)
■ Polyester fiberfill
■ 2 12"/30cm by 16"/41cm polyester pillow forms
■ Size 7 (4.25mm) needles *or size to obtain gauge*
■ Size G/6 (4mm) crochet hook
■ 4½"/11.5cm flat 4-hole white buttons (2 per pillow)
■ Sewing needle and black thread

GAUGE
20 sts and 26 rows to 4"/10cm over St st using size 7 (4.25mm) needles.
Take time to check gauge.

ZEBRA PILLOW
Stripe pattern
Row 1 (RS) With A knit.
Row 2 With A purl.
Row 3 With B knit.
Row 4 With B purl.
Rep rows 1–4.

Body
With A, cast on 120 sts. Work in St st and stripe pat for 16"/41cm, end with row 2 or 4. Bind off.

Legs
(make 4)
With A, cast on 14 sts. Work in garter st for 1"/2.5cm. Join B, beg with row 2 of stripe pat and work even in St st until piece measures 6½"/16.5cm from beg. Bind off.

Head
(make 2)
With A, cast on 14 sts. Work in St st and stripe pat, follow chart for shaping and nose. Bind off.

Ears
(make 2)
With A, cast on 3 sts. Work in St st for 2 rows.
Next (inc) row K1, M1, k to last st, M1, k1—5 sts.
Next row Purl.
Rep last 2 rows once more—7 sts. Work 4 rows even.
Next (dec) row Ssk, k to last 2 sts, k2tog—5 sts.

Next row Purl.

Rep last 2 rows twice more—1 st. Fasten off.

HORSE PILLOW

Body

With C, cast on 120 sts. Work in St st for 16"/41cm. Bind off.

Legs

(make 4)

With A, cast on 14 sts. Work in garter st for 1"/2.5cm. With C, work even in St st until piece measures 6½"/16.5cm from beg. Bind off.

Head

(make 2)

With C, cast on 14 sts. Work in St st, follow chart for shaping and nose. Bind off.

Ears

(make 2)

With C, cast on 3 sts. Work in St st for 2 rows.

Next (inc) row K1, M1, k to last st, M1, k1—5 sts.

Next row Purl.

Rep last 2 rows once more—7 sts. Work 4 rows even.

Next (dec) row Ssk, k to last 2 sts, k2tog—5 sts.

Next row Purl.

Rep last 2 rows twice more—1 st. Fasten off.

FINISHING

Block body piece to measurements.

Fold legs in half lengthwise with RS tog, sew closed leaving cast-on edges open. Turn RS out.

Place both head pieces with RS tog, sew closed leaving bound-off edge open. Turn RS out; attach buttons for eyes as indicated on chart. Fold ears in half and attach to head as indicated on chart. Stuff with fiberfill. Sew rem edge closed.

Fold body in half widthwise with RS tog, zebra's stripes held vertically. Mark fold line for top of pillow and unfold to lay flat with RS facing. Position head at fold line, pointing inward. Allowing for ½"/.5cm seam, position 2 legs at each end of bottom edge, also pointing inward. Refold body with RS tog, head and legs are inside. Sew one side seam closed to attach head and bottom seam to attach legs. Turn body RS out, insert pillow form. Sew rem side seam.

Mane

Cut forty 10"/25.5cm strands of A. With crochet hook, begin at ears and pull each strand through to make fringe (see page 15), working along top edge of head and halfway across back. Trim mane to 4"/10cm.

TAIL

Zebra

Cut three 15"/38cm strands of A. With crochet hook, pull all strands through top corner, opposite head. Fold strands in half and braid together, making one tail strand. Make a knot, leaving 2"/5cm loose at end.

Horse

Cut twelve 17"/43cm strands of A. Fold strands in half. With crochet hook, pull all strands through top corner, opposite head to make fringe (see page 15). Trim to 8"/20cm.

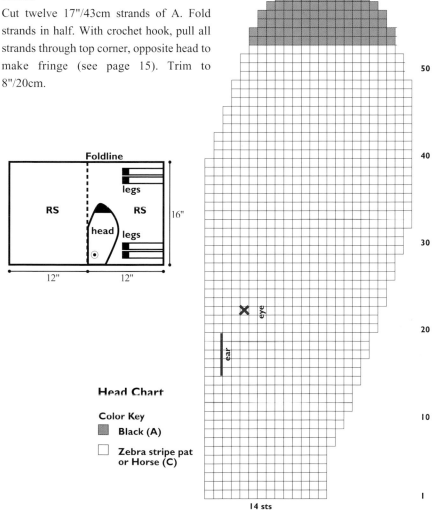

7 sts

60

50

40

30

20

10

1

14 sts

Foldline

legs

RS   RS   16"

head   legs

12"   12"

X   eye

ear

Head Chart

Color Key
- ▨ Black (A)
- ☐ Zebra stripe pat or Horse (C)

Small packages

◀■■■▭

This stunning gift box by Tanis Gray is the knit that keeps on giving. Bestow it on its own or use it as an elegant package for a special treasure. You can never go wrong with two presents in one.

KNITTED MEASUREMENTS

■ 4"/10cm cube

MATERIALS

■ 2 1¾oz/50g (each approx 98yd/90m) skeins Nashua Handknits/Westminster Fibers, Inc. *Creative Focus Kid Mohair* (kid mohair/wool/polyamide) in #18 aqua (⑤)

■ One pair size 8 (5mm) knitting needles *or size to obtain gauge*
■ One pair size 7 (4.5mm) knitting needles
■ Tapestry needle
■ Size 0 (2mm) crochet hook
■ 4"/10cm cardboard gift box with attached lid
■ 2yd/1.8m length of ribbon
■ One button, if desired

GAUGE

16 sts and 20 rows to 4"/10cm over St st using larger needles.
Take time to check gauge.

BOX SIDES

(make 6)

With larger needles, cast on 17 sts. Work in St st until 4½"/11.5cm long.

Bind off purlwise. Block each piece to 4½"/11cm square. With crochet hook, sl st to join pieces following diagram. With knit side facing out, fold into box shape and sl st edges tog.

LINING SIDES

(make 6)

With smaller needles cast on 17 sts. Work in St st until 4"/10cm long.

Bind off purlwise. Block each piece to 4"/10cm square. With crochet hook, sl st to join pieces following diagram. With knit side facing in, fold into box shape and sl st edges tog.

FINISHING

Place knitted lining into cardboard box. Place cardboard box into knitted outer box. With crochet hook, sl st to join boxes, closing all seams.

Tie closed with ribbon. Fasten with button as in photo, if desired.

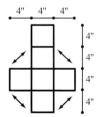

Amelia ear-hat

Diane Zangl's heavenly helmet is worked in the round and features a 2-stitch knit panel between seed stitch sections. A visor adds appeal while two earflaps offer warmth and a bit of modish attitude.

SIZE
Instructions are written for adult's size Medium.

KNITTED MEASUREMENTS
- Circumference 21"/53.5cm
- Length 9½"/24cm

MATERIALS
- 4 1¾oz/50g balls (each approx 36yd/33m) of Dale of Norway *Hubro* (wool) in #4227 cranberry
- Size 8 (5mm) circular needle, 16"/41cm long *or size to obtain gauge*
- One set (4) size 8 (5mm) double-pointed needles (dpns) *or size to obtain gauge*
- Size 7 (4.5mm) needles
- Stitch markers

SEED ST
(worked over an even number of sts)
Rnd 1 *P1, k1; rep from * to end.
Rnd 2 Knit the purl sts and purl the knit sts.
Rep rnd 2 for seed st.

GAUGE
15 sts and 20 rows to 4"/10cm over seed st using size 8 (5mm) needles.

Each 13-st section measures 3½"/9cm.
Take time to check gauge.

HAT
With larger circular needle, cast on 78 sts. Join to work in rnds, taking care not to twist sts. Place marker for end of rnd.
Rnd 1 *K2, [p1, k1] 5 times, k1, place marker; rep from * around—6 sections.
Rnd 2 *K1, [p1, k1] 6 times; rep from * around.
Rep rnds 1 and 2 until hat measures 7"/18cm from beg, end with rnd 2.
Shape crown
Next (dec) rnd *Ssk, work in established seed st to 2 sts before marker, k2tog; rep from * around—66 sts.
Next rnd *K2, work in seed st to marker; rep from * around.
Rep last 2 rnds 4 more times—18 sts.
Next rnd *S2KP; rep from * around—6 sts.
Cut yarn, draw through rem sts twice and pull tightly.
Earflaps
Mark 1 section as center back. With smaller needles and RS facing, work in section to left of center back, pick up and knit 10 sts in purl bumps behind cast-on row.
Slipping first st of every row, knit 11 rows.
Shape ends
Next (dec) row (RS) Sl 1, ssk, k to last 3 sts, k2tog, k1—9 sts.
Next row Sl 1, knit to end of row.

Rep last 2 rows until 5 sts rem.
Next row Sl 1, k3tog, k1—3 sts.

I-CORD TIES
Work 3 rem sts in I-cord (see page 19) until tie measures 6"/15cm. K3tog, fasten off last st. Weave end into cord.
Work second earflap in section on other side center back.

Brim
Mark the center of each of the 3 remaining front sections. With RS facing and smaller needles, beg at first marker, pick up and knit 5 sts in first section, 10 sts in middle section, and 5 sts in third section, end at last marker—20 sts.
Slipping first st of every row, knit 5 rows.

Shape brim
Next (dec) row Ssk, knit to last 2 sts, k2tog—18 sts.
Rep dec row twice—14 sts.
Bind off knitwise on WS.

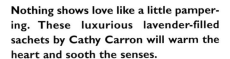

Nothing shows love like a little pampering. These luxurious lavender-filled sachets by Cathy Carron will warm the heart and sooth the senses.

KNITTED MEASUREMENTS

- Approx 4"/10cm wide by 3½"/7.5cm high

MATERIALS

- 1 3½oz/200g ball (each approx 220yd/201m) of Cascade Yarns *220 Heathers* (wool) in #2423 light purple (A), #9453 medium purple (B) and #2421 deep purple (C) 🔲
- One set (4) size 6 (4mm) double-pointed needles (dpns) *or size to obtain gauge*
- Small bag of dried lavender buds
- Three small muslin bags, each approx 4"/10cm wide and 3½"/7.5cm high
- Yarn needle
- Sewing needle and thread
- 18"/46cm of ½"/1.5cm-wide satin ribbon

SEED ST SACHET

GAUGE
10 sts and 8 rows to 2"/5cm over seed st.
Take time to check gauge.

Seed st
Rnd 1 *K1, p1; rep from * around.
Rnd 2 Knit the purl sts and purl the knit sts.
Rep rnd 2 for seed st.
With A cast on 40 sts, distribute over 3 dpns. Join to work in rnds, taking care not to twist sts. Place marker for end of rnd. Work in seed st until piece measures 3½"/7.5cm long. Bind off.

BASKETWEAVE ST SACHET

GAUGE
10 sts and 14 rows to 2"/10cm over basketweave st.
Take time to check gauge.

Basketweave st
Rnds 1—4 *K4, p4; rep from * around.
Rnds 5—8 *P4, k4; rep from * around.
Rep rnds 1–8 for basketweave st.
With B, cast on 40 sts, distribute over 3 dpns. Join to work in rnds, taking care not to twist sts. Place marker for end of rnd.
Work in basketweave st until piece measures 3½"/7.5cm, end with rnd 4 or 8. Bind off.

ANDALUSIAN ST SACHET

GAUGE
9 sts and 16 rows to 2"/5cm over Andalusian st.
Take time to check gauge.

Andalusian st
Rnds 1—3 Knit.
Rnd 4 *K1, p1; rep from * around.
Rep rnds 1–4 for Andalusian st.
With C, cast on 40 sts, distribute over 3 dpns. Join to work in rnds, taking care not to twist sts. Place marker for end of rnd.
Work in Andalusian st until piece measures

3½"/7.5cm, end with rnd 3. Bind off.

FINISHING

Fill each muslin bag with lavender, sew closed. With matching yarn, sew one end of each knitted sachet closed. Insert bag, sew top closed. Stack the 3 sachets, wrap with ribbon and tie a bow.

Know a tech wizard who s always on the go? Tanis Gray s cool-toned laptop bag features a convenient front pocket and a sturdy structure that will stand up to daily commutes, endless library trips and airport security with stylish ease.

KNITTED MEASUREMENTS
- 18½"/47cm wide by 20½"/52cm tall before felting
- 14"/35.5cm wide by 10½"/26.5cm tall after felting

MATERIALS
- 4 3½oz/100g skeins (each approx 138yd/126m) Manos del Uruguay/ Fairmount Fibers, Ltd. *Handspun Multi Colors* (wool) in #116 caribe (MC) ⑤
- 1 1¾oz/50g skein (each approx 114yd/110m) Koigu Wool Designs *Kersti* (wool) in #2339 lime ③
- One pair size 11 (8mm) knitting needles *or size needed to obtain gauge*
- Tapestry needle
- One 1"/2.5cm button
- Sewing needle and thread

GAUGE
14 sts and 13 rows to 4"/10cm over St st using size 11 (8mm) needles before felting. *Take time to check gauge.*

FRONT
With MC cast on 56 sts. Work in St st until piece measures 20½"/52cm from beg—67 rows. Bind off.

BACK
Cast on and work as for front until same length as back, end with WS row.
Next row (RS) Bind off 19 sts, k18, bind off rem sts.

FLAP
Reattach yarn and work even on 18 sts for 6"/15cm. Bind off.

POCKET
Cast on and work as for front until piece measures 10½"/27cm from beg—35 rows. Bind off.

FINISHING
With RS tog, sew front and back together along cast-on edge and side seams.
Place front/back and pocket each in separate mesh bags or pillowcases and felt in washing machine (see page 14).
Turn front/back right side out. Gently pull pieces into shape and let dry.
Cut small hole into flap for button at 1"/2.5cm from bound-off edge.
With A sew around buttonhole using blanket stitch (see page 19).
Sew button onto front, approx 1"/2.5cm from top edge.
With sewing needle and thread, sew pocket to front. With A work blanket st around top edge of front/back, around flap and across top of pocket.

■■■■▭

Quick to knit, tot-sized and just plain precious, Lucinda Guy's lovable stuffed chick is sure to become your little one's constant companion.

■ Approx 5"/13cm tall

MATERIALS
■ 1 1¾oz/50g ball (each approx 124yd/113m) of Rowan Yarns/ Westminster Fibers, Inc., Wool Cotton (wool/cotton) in #964 still (MC) and #955 ship shape (A) ⬛❸⬛
■ Small amount #943 flower (B)
■ Size 6 (4mm) needles *or size to obtain gauge*
■ Sewing needle and thread
■ Polyester fiberfill

GAUGE
22 sts and 30 rows to 4"/10cm over St st using size 6 (4mm) needles.
Take time to check gauge.

BODY
(make 2)
With MC cast on 26 sts.
Work 26 rows in St st.
Next (dec) rnd (RS) K1, SKP, knit to last 3 sts, SKP, k1—24 sts.
Work even for 3 rows.
Rep dec row every RS row 3 times more— 18 sts.

Bind off.

BOTTOM AND CHEST
With MC cast on 3 sts.
Knit 1 row, purl 1 row.
Next (inc) row (RS) K into back and front of first and last st—5 sts.
Next row Purl.
Rep last 2 rows 5 times more—15 sts.
Work even in St st until piece measures 4½"/11.5cm from beg and fits along cast-on edge of body.
Next (dec) row (RS) K1, SKP, knit to last 3 sts, SKP, k1—13 sts.
Work even for 3 rows.
Rep dec row every fourth row 4 times more—5 sts.
Next (dec) row (RS) K2tog, k1, k2tog—3 sts.
Work 3 rows even. Bind off.

FRONT WING
(make 2)
With A cast on 10 sts.
Work 10 rows in St st.
Next (inc) row K into back and front of first st, k to end—11 sts.
Purl 1 row.
Next row K into back and front of first st, k to last 3 sts, SKP, k1—11 sts.
Purl 1 row.
Rep last 2 rows once more.
Next (dec) row (RS) K to last 3 sts, SKP, k1—10 sts.

Next (dec) row (WS) P2tog, p to last 2 sts, p2tog—8 sts.
Bind off.

(make 2)
With A cast on 10 sts.
Work 10 rows in St st.
Next (inc) row K across to last st, k into back and front of last st—11 sts.
Purl 1 row.
Next row K1, SKP, k across to last st, k into back and front of last st—11 sts.
Purl 1 row.
Rep last two rows once more.
Next (dec) row (RS) K1, SKP, k to end—10 sts.
Next (dec) row (WS) P2tog, p to last 2 sts, p2tog—8 sts.
Bind off.

TAIL
(make 2)
With A cast on 6 sts.
Work 2 rows in St st.
Next (inc) row K into back and front of first st, k across, knit into back and front of last st—8 sts.
Work 3 rows in St st.
Rep inc row every fourth row twice more—12 sts. Work 5 rows in St st. Bind off.

BEAK
(make 2)
With A cast on 7 sts.
Work 2 rows in St st.
Next (dec) row K1, SKP, knit to last 3 sts, SKP, k1—5 sts.
Purl 1 row.
Next (dec) row K2tog, k1, k2tog—3 sts.
Purl 1 row.
Next (dec) row K3 sts tog—1 st.
Fasten off.

FINISHING
Press all pieces on WS using a warm iron over a damp cloth.

Wings
Match front and back wings with RS facing tog, sew all edges closed except cast-on edge. Turn RS out, fill with fiberfill and sew closed.

Tail
Match tail pieces, with RS facing tog, sew all edges closed except cast-on edge. Turn RS out, fill with fiberfill and sew closed.

Beak
Match beak pieces, with RS facing tog, sew closed except cast-on edge. Turn RS out, fill with fiberfill and sew closed.

Assembly
With RS facing tog, sew two pieces of body closed along bound-off edge for top of bird.

With A duplicate st eyes foll diagram (see page 14). With B work French knots (see page 19) on the body and chest.

Position the fasten-off end of chest/underbody at the top seam, between the body pieces. Ease the chest/underbody to fit along the side and bottom edges of body. Sew in place, leaving rem body side open. Sew beak to chest/underbody, positioning just below eye level. Sew wings to body sides, positioning 2"/5cm down from top edge and in middle of body. Fill bird with fiberfill. Sew rem side edge closed. Attach tail to bottom of body and sew to side seam for reinforcement.

Eyes

  Stitch Key

 Duplicate st with B

RESOURCES

Write to the yarn companies listed below for purchasing and mail-order information.

Brown Sheep Company
100662 County Road 16
Mitchell, NE 69357
www.brownsheep.com

Cascade Yarns
1224 Andover Park East
Tukwila, WA 98188
www.cascadeyarns.com

Classic Elite Yarns
122 Western Avenue
Lowell, MA 01851
www.classiceliteyarns.com

Claudia Hand Painted Yarns
40 West Washington Street
Harrisonburg, VA 22802
www.claudiaco.com

Cleckheaton
distributed by
Plymouth Yarn Co.

Dale of Norway
4750 Shelburne Road
Shelburne, VT 05482
www.dale.no

Fairmount Fibers, Ltd.
915 North 28th Street
Philadelphia, PA 19130
www.fairmountfibers.com

Frog Tree Yarn
14 Frog Tree Lane
East Dennis, MA 02641
www.frogtreeyarn.com

JCA, Inc.
35 Scales Lane
Townsend, MA 01469
www.jcacrafts.com

Lion Brand Yarn
34 West 15th Street
New York, NY 10011
www.lionbrand.com

Louet Sales
808 Commerce Park Drive
Ogdensburg, NY 13669

Manos del Uruguay
distributed by
Fairmount Fibers, Ltd.
www.manos.com.uy

Nashua Handknits
distributed by
Westminster Fibers, Inc.

Plymouth Yarn Co.
P.O. Box 28
Bristol, PA 19007
www.plymouthyarn.com

Reynolds
distributed by
JCA, Inc.

Rowan Yarns
distributed by
Westminster Fibers, Inc.
www.knitrowan.com

Schulana
distributed by Skacel
Collection, Inc.

Skacel Collection, Inc.
P.O. Box 88110
Seattle, WA 98138
www.skacelknitting.com

Westminster Fibers
165 Ledge Street
Nashua, NH 03060
www.westminsterfibers.com

U.K. RESOURCES

Not all yarns used in this book are available in the U.K. For yarns not available, make a comparable substitute or contact the U.S. manufacturer for purchasing and mail-order information.

Green Lane Mill
Holmfirth
HD9 2DX England
www.knitrowan.com

CANADIAN RESOURCES

Write to U.S. resources for mail-order availability of yarns not listed.

Bernat
320 Livingstone Avenue
South
Listowel, Ontario
Canada N4W 3H3
www.bernat.com

Koigu Wool Designs
Box 158
563295 Glenelg Holland
Townline
Chatsworth, Ontario
Canada N0H 1G0
www.koigu.com

Louet Sales
R.R. 4
Prescott, Ontario
Canada K0E 1T0
www.louet.com

Patons
320 Livingstone Avenue
South
Listowel, Ontario
Canada N4W 3H3
www.patonsyarns.com

VOGUE KNITTING QUICK GIFTS

Editorial Director
ELAINE SILVERSTEIN

Book Division Manager
ERICA SMITH

Executive Editor
CARLA S. SCOTT

Associate Editor
AMANDA KEISER

Art Director
CHI LING MOY

Associate Art Director
SHEENA T. PAUL

Yarn Editor
TANIS GRAY

Instructions Editors
LISA BUCCELLATO
VICTORIA HILDITCH

Photography
JACK DEUTSCH STUDIO

Copy Editor
KRISTINA SIGLER

■

Vice President, Publisher
TRISHA MALCOLM

Production Manager
DAVID JOINNIDES

Creative Director
JOE VIOR

President
ART JOINNIDES

LOOK FOR THESE OTHER TITLES IN THE *VOGUE KNITTING ON THE GO!* SERIES...

■